Keep Them Thinking

· Level III ·

A Handbook of Model Lessons

James Bellanca

SKYLIGHT PUBLISHING, INC.
Palatine, Illinois

Other titles in this series:

Keep Them Thinking: Level I (grades K-3)
Keep Them Thinking: Level II (grades 4-9)

Start Them Thinking (grades K-3)
Catch Them Thinking (grades 4-12)
Teach Them Thinking (grades K-12)

The Thinking Log (grades K-6)
The Thinking/Writing Connection (grades 6-12)

Keep Them Thinking: Level III
First Printing

Published by Skylight Publishing, 200 E. Wood Street, Suite 250, Palatine, Illinois 60067

Editing: Robin Fogarty, Sharon Nowakowski
Type Composition and Formatting: Donna Ramirez
Book Design and Formatting: Bruce Leckie
Illustrations: Jim Arthur

Printed in the United States of America
ISBN# 0-932935-06-0

Foreword

Our children are the messages we send to a time we will not see.
—Betty Seigle

The lessons in this series are designed with three premises in mind: The teacher is the architect of the intellect, the student is the capable apprentice and thinking is more basic than the basics—it frames all learning.

Premise 1 — The Teacher Is The Architect Of The Intellect

A teacher affects eternity. He never knows where his influence ends.

—Henry Adams

As an architect of the intellect, a teacher leaves his mark on history. The classroom teacher is, above all else, a designer of learning, an expert craftsman who knows content, understands child development, and manages young people with finesse.

The excellent teacher skillfully crafts the lesson with a clear purpose. Just as form follows function for the traditional architect, the structure of the lesson is determined by the learning goal.

Aesthetically, lessons are designed to invite the learner in. When the design is exquisite, the invitation becomes irresistible to the learner. He enters the learning situation excited and with a level of expectancy that sets the scene for motivated learning.

Premise 2 — The Student Is The Capable Apprentice

Come to the edge, he said. They said: We are afraid.
Come to the edge, he said. They came.
He pushed them...and they flew.

—Apollinaire

Believing that the student is capable of becoming the master of his own learning is sometimes difficult for the architect mentor. But through carefully crafted instruction, exemplary, consistent modeling and deliberate practice, the apprentice learns. Only then, by relinquishing the honored role of master architect, is the student free to advance on his own.

To believe one is capable is to let go. It is to trust and to watch as the learner takes over—and goes beyond—for he is the capable apprentice.

Premise 3   Thinking Is More Basic Than The Basics

Intelligent behavior is knowing what to do when you don't know what to do.

—Arthur Costa

Thinking is the foundation for all learning. To say we're going to teach thinking in our classroom does not imply that we don't already do just that. Of course we teach thinking, but now by focusing on cognitive behavior, thinking becomes the blueprint by which we design and structure learning.

The blueprint of thinking becomes the reference that guides our instructional decisions. And, as the architect of the intellect, we concern ourselves as much with the process as with the final product. We select materials with care and deliberation. We direct activities with skill and closely monitor the progress. Finally, with a feeling of pride and accomplishment, we stand back and view the masterpiece—in this case a cadre of young people—thinking and learning in self-directed ways.

Robin Fogarty
Editor

Contents

Foreword iii

Introduction vii

Creative Thinking Skill: Scoring Goals! 1
Explicit Skill Model Lesson 2
Short Practices 11
Transfer Lesson in Literature 12
Transfer Lesson in Study Skills 15
Evaluation of Skills 17

Critical Thinking Skill: Analyzing for Cause and Effect 19
Explicit Skill Model Lesson 20
Short Practices 31
Transfer Lesson in Social Issues 33
Transfer Lesson in Science 35
Transfer Lesson in History 37
Evaluation of Skills 40

Problem-Solving Skill: Analytic Problem-Solving for Solutions 41
Explicit Skill Model Lesson 42
Short Practices 53
Transfer Lesson in Literature 58
Transfer Lesson in History 61
Transfer Lesson in Science 63
Evaluation of Skills 65

Masters Appendix 67
Premise 1 68
Premise 2 69
Premise 3 70
ABC's of Goal Setting 71
Newspaper Basketball Rules 72
Types of Goals 73
Goal Clarifying Questions 74
DOVE Rules for Brainstorming 75
Goal Clarifying Checklist 76
Evaluation of Skills: Scoring Goals! 77
Problem Topic List 78
Making a Pro-Con Chart 79
Evaluation of Skills: Analyzing for Cause and Effect 80

The Creative People Search 81
The Problem Scenarios 82
Project Planning Worksheet 83
Sample Article: Viral Map 84
Evaluation of Skills: Analytic Problem-Solving for Solutions 85

Worksheet Model for Original Lessons 87

Bibliography 90

Introduction

Keep Them Thinking: Level III presents thinking lessons and activities designed especially for students in grades 7 through 12. Although many of these students have not had explicit training in creative and critical thinking, they are frequently expected to perform tasks that require analytic or evaluative skills. Additionally, to be successful in the various academic content areas, students must be adept at generating and producing ideas. Therefore, it is pertinent that these young people master both critical and creative thinking.

To ease students into a thinking curriculum, three fully developed thinking lessons are conveniently outlined for immediate classroom use.

Creative Thinking

In the first section, **"Scoring Goals,"** students learn creative and generative thinking skills while using the guidelines for formal brainstorming. They practice setting goals that are achievable, believable and conceivable.

Critical Thinking

Critical, analytical and mental processing is required in **"Analyzing for Cause and Effect."** This section revolves around real-life scenarios to provide motivation and relevance for intense student involvement.

Problem Solving

In the third section, **"Analytic Problem-Solving for Solutions,"** real-life, controversial scenarios are used as the vehicles to explore analytic problem-solving. Students learn how to use graphic organizers to chart and plan solutions to problems.

Explicit Lessons

Each of the three focus skills are developed around a similar format. You will find an explicit teaching model with highlighted information and notes. This elaborated model provides a prototype or template for you to adopt in designing other explicit thinking skill lessons, practice exercises and transfer activities to follow up or enhance the ones already outlined in each lesson.

The **Model Lessons** Include:

Lesson Objective The skill for the lesson explicitly stated; you may want to post this on the chalkboard or a signpost before each lesson.

Key Vocabulary Vocabulary that may require clarification, explanation and/or emphasis before, during and after the lesson.

Looking Back A brief statement to stir prior knowledge and to help relate the new information to previous experiences.

Getting Ready Background information, rationale and premises that undergird the lesson.

At-A-Glance A synopsis of the lesson or the lesson in a nutshell.

Materials Needed A quick reference list of all the materials you will need for the model lesson.

Focus Activity A short anticipatory activity suggested to set the stage for the introduction of the new skill.

Activity Objective A concise statement of the purpose of the main activity.

Activity The interactive part of the classroom lesson, including the instructional input and the student participation.

Metacognitive Processing Reflective questions, activities and discussion ideas about the lesson and the new skill.

Practice

To ensure internalization of the skills, short practices are outlined after the model lesson. The **Short Practices** offer suggestions for using the skills in your lessons and provide examples of exercises for relating that skill to familiar situations in students' everyday lives.

Transfer

Specifically tailored to activities in a variety of subject areas, the **Transfer Lessons** delineate the ease of bridging thinking skills across the curriculum. These shortened versions of the model lesson include: **Focus Activity**, **Objective**, **Activity**, **Structured Discussion**, **Metacognitive Processing** and **Follow-up** (lesson extensions and enrichment ideas for both in and out of the classroom).

Evaluation of Skills

As a final step in ensuring student transfer and understanding of the thinking skills presented, each chapter concludes with an **Evaluation of Skills**. You may use this section to further process the activities with your students or to measure, gauge or evaluate you students' development and comprehension of the lessons.

Ongoing Transfer

View the lessons as generic patterns upon which to model personally relevant lesson plans for the teaching of critical and creative thinking. Enjoy the activities and their flexibility in teaching students cognitive skills as thinking becomes an integral part of all that we do in our interactions with students.

Creative Thinking Level III

Scoring Goals!

Thinking Skill: *Scoring Goals!*

We must ask where we are and whither we are tending.
—Abraham Lincoln

Model Lesson:

Lesson Objective To identify the factors involved in setting realistic goals.

Key Vocabulary Goals, strategies, achievable, believable, capable, real, clarify, focus, support, extend.

Looking Back Everyone has felt out of place at one time or another. Yet, all people have certain people, places, sounds, etc. that make them feel comfortable and at ease. Children sometimes have a favorite place to read or a favorite doll to talk to; they even have special places for sleeping and playing. Successful businesses also have found that setting the right climate and atmosphere is the key to efficient production. Teachers too have already discovered that setting the climate for students to begin thinking is very beneficial—i.e., keeping the noise to an acceptable level, having runners walk, accepting no fighting, and offering encouraging words and gestures. With the nurturing classroom climate in place, students are ready to stretch their learning—within the classroom and beyond schoolyard experiences—because scoring goals is a life-long quest.

Getting Ready In a society that has instant gratification as the norm, looking ahead, planning, taking risks, developing strategies and stretching one's self-expectations are not commonly mastered skills. It is far easier for most students to follow the TV model and constantly react to the instant impulse. Without the ability to look ahead, to set realistic goals and to plan alternate strategies, few students will become critical thinkers who analyze situations and develop creative solutions. Setting goals is the foundation of strong problem solving. Students who learn to set *achievable*, *believable* and *capable* goals are students well down the road to becoming realistic and successful problem solvers. Realistic problem-solving begins with the A, B and C of goal setting—A=achievable, B=believable and C=capable. These are three criteria that can help students measure the quality of their goals. Consider each.

Achievable: An achievable goal is one that the individual can trace, step by step, from his/her current place to the actual attainment—the goal is clear and explicit. On the long climb to the goal, the individual knows each step in sequence, which steps are critical and which steps may need some adjusting. For instance, Sue, an outstanding 15-year-old tennis player, wants to reach her goal— to play professional tennis. She has thought carefully about what she must do. She knows, for instance, that she must practice a minimum of four hours per day, continue her weight program, control her diet as prescribed by the team nutritionist, strengthen her serve, and so on. By breaking her long-range goal into manageable, sequenced steps, she makes her goal more *achievable*.

Believable: A believable goal is one which is built on a careful assessment of what is within our grasp. All students need to use their personal experiences to refine their visions of what is possible or what is within their grasp. Direct experience can be the best teacher; indirect experience also helps. For instance, Sue may wish to be a professional tennis player, but for Sue's mother, that goal is not very believable. Sue's mother has never read about, saw on TV or at the movies nor heard about a woman becoming a pro tennis player. The dream is virtually *unbelievable* because she has never seen any concrete models. Sue, however, has read about women pros in *Sports Illustrated*, seen women's tennis at Wimbleton attended a pro tournament at Forest Hills, got Steffi Graf's autograph, and interviewed her next-door neighbor, a pro women's tennis coach, for the high school paper. Sue's first-hand contact with women pros makes her goal *believable*.

Capable: A capable goal is one built on solid assessment of one's strengths and weaknesses. The assessment is solid to the degree that good evidence from reliable sources is available to tell students what they can and cannot do. Sue's coach is a reliable source. Every week she previews a videotape of Sue's practices. Together they keep a tally of how well Sue does with each type of shot. They measure her strengths, accuracy and attention. They can compare her skills to others in her ability class as well as to women pros to evaluate her *capability*.

The ABC's of goal setting help students clarify their goals and bring them into a line that is more realistic. When taken together, the ABC's help students form a more realistic, intertwined picture of what is desired and the best means to that goal. By learning to use the ABC approach, teachers give students a tool that sets a very positive and clarifying framework for substantive problem-solving.

At-A-Glance You will introduce students to the concept of goal setting with a focus activity that challenges them to reach a pre-set goal. As a team, two students will determine the amount of risk they will take to make the best score in a game competition. As they discuss their decisions and the results of the activity, you will introduce the vocabulary with appropriate examples. You will introduce an interview task in which partners will select goal clarifying questions and personal goals. Finally, you will select transfer activities so students may practice the clarification of goals in their academic, social, work and athletic situations.

Focus Activity

1. Set up the room before students enter. Put the **Activity Objective** on the board (or signpost). To set up the room, place all the chairs in a *U* facing the front. In the mouth of the *U*, place the waste can.

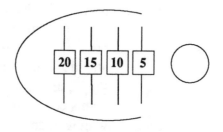

Materials Needed

☐ Newsprint, tape and markers

☐ A large waste can

☐ Cards labeled 5, 10, 15, etc.

☐ Newspaper basketballs

☐ ABC's of Goal Setting (transparency)

☐ Newspaper Basketball Rules (handout or transparency)

☐ Goal Clarifying Questions (handout)

☐ Thinking Logs

2. Using three-foot strips of masking tape, mark lines four feet apart, from the waste can to the bottom of the *U*. Place tent cards marked 5, 10, 15, etc. on the lines, starting with the 5 card on the line nearest the waste can. These cards indicate the score earned for a successful toss from each line.

3. After the students are seated, divide them into pairs with someone they haven't worked with recently. Give each pair a newspaper basketball. Using a previously prepared piece of newsprint, review the rules.

Newspaper Basketball Rules

I. Everyone gets a partner. The two of them are a team. Each team, one at a time, makes three throws. One partner throws and the other one retrieves. Three throws comprise a team's round.

II. The only way to score points during the rounds is by throwing the newspaper basketball into the waste can. The score for each "basket" is determined by the line from which a player throws it.

III. Before starting a round, each team predicts what its final score for the round will be. Each team must write down and announce its predicted score to the class. In addition, each team must announce which lines it will attempt its three throws from to reach its predicted score.

IV. Teams may attempt to make all throws from behind one line or from a variety of lines. Each team is responsible for keeping its own working score during its round.

V. At the end of a round, the team's score is recorded on the official score sheet. After all teams have had a round, the team with the highest score wins. Play-off rounds may be necessary to break first-place ties.

---

4. Before starting the rounds, give each pair three minutes to determine the score it wants to reach and the lines it will throw from to reach that score. Take the teams in a pre-announced sequence. Each team must declare its predicted point-goal score and the lines it will use to achieve that score.

5. Rotate the teams so that all get to throw. After the last team has finished, add the scores and rank the top 10 teams.

	Round #1 Total Points	Rank #1	Round #2 Total Points	Rank #2
Team #1	15	#2		
Team #2	5	#3		
Team #3	25	#1		

6. Allow each team three to five minutes to evaluate its goal, strategy and results. Allow another two minutes for the teams to prepare for the next round. If they decide to change their goals or strategies, they must be prepared to explain their reasons.

7. Repeat the round.

8. After all teams are finished and they have time to evaluate their performances, ask them to raise their hands in response to these questions. A raised hand will indicate a yes; a hand kept down means no.

    a. How many teams achieved both of the goals they set? one of the goals?

    b. How many fell short of their goals? overachieved or went beyond?

    c. How many were more accurate the first time? the second?

    d. How many made a change the second time? What were the reasons? Did it help?

9. Write this lead-in on the board:

    In doing this goal task, I learned . . . .

    Allow students a few moments to reflect and then whip around the *U* for in-turn responses. Allow students to say, "I pass."

Activity Objective To identify the factors that go into making realistic goals.

Activity Point to the objective on the board and then underline the words *realistic* and *goals*. Review the **Focus Activity** and show them that the scores they set out to achieve were their goals. Ask them to identify other games in which they must pick a goal to win. Next, identify goals that a person might have that are not part of winning but are important anyway. After you have some examples, introduce the word *realistic*. Ask many students to share with the class what that word means to them. Honor their answers and share with them how hard it is to explain such a word. Explain that when it comes to goals, however, we can use some other words to help us understand the word *realistic*. Use the ABC's of Goal Setting transparency to review successful goal setting..

1. Match the students into groups of three. Identify which student got out of bed the earliest this morning in each trio. That person will go last. The person to the early bird's right will go first, the next person will go second.

2. Introduce the words *clarify*, *extend*, *focus* and *support* by writing them on the board or overhead. Solicit several explanations and examples of each word. Instruct the students to make a vocabulary list of these words in their logs.

3. The first person is the focus person. The focus person may select one of the following goals to share with his/her group:

TYPES OF GOALS

a career goal

a skill goal

an academic achievement goal

a product goal

a task goal

a personal relationship goal

a personal improvement goal

a family goal

a spiritual goal

a physical achievement goal

a travel goal

The focus person describes his/her goal as specifically as possible in three minutes. The focus person may wish to describe the reasons for the goal, the advantages, how it was selected, what benefits it might bring, the hardships that it presents, etc.

4. The other two members in the group offer their complete attention on the focus person for six minutes. For the first three minutes, the focus person describes the goal with no interruptions from the others; one of the listeners keeps time. For the next three minutes, the two listeners alternate asking extending questions from the Goal Clarifying Questions handout, to draw out the focus person. See the following page for examples of the Goal Clarifying Questions. (You may want to keep a poster of these questions in the room.) In no way are listeners to argue with the focus person. They should use good eye contact, positive body language and give non-verbal support to that person's responses. All questions must come from the ABC list unless it is necessary for the listeners to ask a clarifying question such as "Can you be more specific?" or "Can you give us an example?" Questions such as "Why?" and "Don't you think . . . ?" are *out of bounds*.

GOAL CLARIFYING QUESTIONS

A = Achievable

What are the steps you will have to take to accomplish this goal?

Can you sequence them?

Which are the three most critical steps? Why?

Which are the least important?

Which steps may need some adjusting? Which will cause you to adjust your own ideals, beliefs, habits or lifestyle?

How ready are you to make adjustments to reach your goal?

What will you not change or give up?

What are the major external blocks in your path?

How will you handle these?

What resources do you have that can help you? How will you use them?

What is the major hurdle? Which resource will help the most in overcoming that hurdle?

B = Believable

What experiences have you had that will help you achieve your goal?

Which are most critical? How will they help?

What models do you have in thinking you can reach this goal?

What tangible evidence will you have to tell you that you are successful?

What means do you have to critique your progress, give feedback and check your assumptions about yourself?

C = Capable

What personal strengths do you have that will help you achieve your goal?

What are the limits within yourself that will hinder you?

How do you plan to deal with your limits? use your strengths?

What alternatives have you considered? Are any possible?

Can you influence persons who can assist you? What do you intend to do?

5. Review the ABC concept of clarifying goals (see the explanation in **Getting Ready**). After you have given your explanation of each word, ask several different students to put the concept into their own words and give examples from their own experiences. Practice wait time and reinforce their good thinking.

6. Conduct a model interview by selecting a goal area from your life and sharing it with the class. Have a timekeeper stop you after three minutes. Invite students to select questions from the list for you to answer. Don't forget, you also have the right to say, "I pass." (In fact, this is a good chance to model that it's OK to pass.) After three or four questions, check for understanding of the focus interview instructions by asking for thumbs up (for 100 percent understanding), thumbs sideways (for partial understanding) and thumbs down (for completely lost). Clarify as needed, having students who signaled thumbs up help clarify and someone who answered thumbs down give a final recap or explanation. Put the groups to work for the first round.

7. At the end of the six minutes, instruct the focus person to give a specific "I appreciate . . ." statement to each partner for the assistance provided. Also, have each focus person write in his/her log the original goal statement and any change made because of the clarification and support from a partner.

8. While the first focus person is completing the log entry, the others may prepare their goal statements. When you signal, the next person in the group becomes the focus person. Continue the round using the same procedures as in the first round of interviewing. When the second focus person's log entry is done, the third person moves to focus and completes the final round.

Metacognitive Processing
Using a classroom wrap-around, ask students to respond in turn to the following processing lead-in:

From this goal clarifying activity, I learned . . . .

Encourage all to listen carefully to the ideas; ask volunteers to identify the similarities. Have a student list these on newsprint or the blackboard. When several are listed, seek multiple responses to the following questions:

What conclusions can you draw from this list of similarities? Why?

What general statements can you make about the worth or value of asking goal clarifying questions?

What might be some appropriate times or situations for you to ask yourself goal clarifying questions?

After hearing several responses, instruct the students to write in their logs one appropriate question they might ask themselves in each of the three ABC areas. They may pick a different goal from the one they previously discussed in the **Activity**.

Short Practices:

The following practices give guided reinforcement for the ABC criteria. Students can review questions from the worksheet and think through the criteria for use in their real-life challenges as well as in mock situations. Additional short practices, which follow the models used here, may be necessary for some classes. So that all students become skilled at using the goal clarifying questions in their own thinking, it is important that after each practice the students focus on the ABC's and make direct connections to their own metacognitive goal processing.

■ Group students in threes. Provide each group of three with an article selected by you from the daily newspaper. Have one student read the article to his/her group. After the reading, instruct the students to identify the major goal for each person or group in the story. Model an example. Using the Goal Clarifying Questions handout, each group should select one question to ask from each of the three areas. Finally, have each group set up a role play in which one person narrates the story, one person acts as a news journalist on TV and asks the questions, and the third responds as the character would. Select several role plays for presentation to the class. After the presentations, ask the students to explain why they selected the particular questions they used.

■ Every day for a week assign all students to select a new type of goal from the Types of Goals handout. Tell them to select three questions that will help them clarify their new goal and to write out their responses. The next day, have students return to their support groups or assigned groupings. Tell students that each group member is to take two minutes in turn to share his new goal and the responses he wrote to his clarifying questions. By the end of the week, students will have had the chance to think about a variety of life goals that pertain directly to them. They will see the variety of goals in their own lives as well as compared with others' goals in their groups.

Transfer Lesson:
Looking At Literature

Focus Activity Have students complete one of the following lead-ins in their logs:

An important academic goal for me this week is . . . .

It will benefit me in the following ways . . . .

An important personal goal that will benefit me this week

is . . . .

I will benefit because . . . .

Allow two to four minutes for students to complete the task. Review the key vocabulary from the lesson as well as the ABC's. Remember to have wait time and an equal distribution of student responses.

Objective To practice the goal clarifying questions using literature and popular mass media.

Activity

1. Select a short story, film, novel or biography and assign it to the class.

2. After the class has read/viewed the assigned selection, put students into study groups of four. Identify the person born latest in the year. That person is the recorder for the first day. The next latest birthday is the leader for the first day. The next latest birthday handles the materials. The person with the earliest birthday keeps time and observes. All jobs rotate one person to the right each day.

3. Tell the class that each group will receive three grades, one for how they promote thinking together, one for the final product

and one for their knowledge of the ABC's of goal clarifying. All groups are responsible for turning in all newsprint, the final assignment and the group's test result.

4. In preparation for the activity, have all group leaders review DOVE, the helpful thinking conditions, the role responsibilities and the task instructions after they are presented by the teacher. The materials manager prepares the newsprint, markers, etc.

   DOVE is a strategy to promote formal brainstorming. Its letters represent the following:

   DOVE

   Defer judgment—accept all ideas, list everything, evaluate later

   Opt for original—anything goes, especially different and crazy ideas

   Vast numbers of ideas are best—get many ideas, the more the better

   Expand by association—piggyback off of each other's ideas

   The DOVE strategy is referred to again and again throughout this book. You may want to keep a poster of the strategies in your classroom for students to use as a guide throughout the year. The rules and ideas presented in DOVE can help students remember to keep an open mind in scoring goals, solving problems, analyzing situations and much more. Remember to reinforce the DOVE guidelines in all your lessons for which students brainstorm ideas.

5. Assign one main character from the story to each group. Using in-turn responses, each group lists a character's major goals. After listing each goal, the group clarifies the goal by reviewing the appropriate events and label it according to the Types of Goals handout. After all proposed goals are reviewed and labeled, each person selects the one he/she believes is most important in the character's life in the story. Do not duplicate choices. Each group should end with four selections for the character. Give an example.

6. Have the groups choose which scenario they each will create to interview their characters: the network news, a radio talk show, a morning TV talk show, the Johnny Carson show, etc. The groups should have a narrator, a host, the character, a director with props, etc. Allow time for each group to prepare an on-air interview of its character by the celebrity host. At least half of the questions must come from the ABC Goal Clarifying Questions handout. Encourage the groups to be original. After each skit, the cast should explain its reasons for the questions as well as the character's responses.

Structured Discussion
In the logs, have students rephrase the meanings of *achievable*, *believable* and *capable*. On the board, make three columns, each headed by one of the words. Ask for nominations, seconds and a simple majority vote for the most achievable, most believable and most capable goal/character. Take no more than three nominations for each heading. After the nominations are closed, start with the first word, *achievable*. Have all students supporting the first nomination gather in one corner of the room, those supporting the second nomination in a second corner, and those favoring the third in the third corner. Next, have each group select a recorder to write down all the supportive reasons for that nominee. After three minutes, allow each group to argue its case in turn. When all three have presented the arguments, regroup for the second arguments for the word *believable*. Repeat the process of identifying the arguments and presenting the case. Move to the final column, *capable*, and repeat the process. No one may serve as a recorder or a reporter more than once in this round.

Metacognitive Processing
Conclude this goal clarifying practice with a log entry. Invite students to reflect on the goal clarifying questions they used. In their logs, students should enter three goal clarifying questions that are especially valuable to their academic goals.

Follow-Up
Assign students to interview adults about their goals, either their goals as an adult or goals from throughout their lives. Have the students select questions from the Goal Clarifying Checklist. Tabulate and contrast students' results and responses in class the next day.

Or, invite a business person, official or athlete to the classroom. Have the students prepare goal clarifying questions. Ask the speaker to discuss his/her life successes in relation to important goals. Allow time for students' questions.

Transfer Lesson:
Study Skills Sampler

Focus Activity Tell each student to select one course that he/she is taking this year. Students should select one area in their courses—reading, writing, taking notes, preparing for tests, participating in class, etc.—that they feel needs improvement. In the log, have students write a 75-word tentative goal statement for that improvement. It might read, "By the end of the first quarter, I will have entered 300 words into my vocabulary log." Get other examples from students.

After the students have completed the draft of their study skill goals, provide the Goal Clarifying Checklist transparency, poster or handout (see checklist below). Students can use the checklist to review their statements.

GOAL CLARIFYING CHECKLIST	
Does your statement indicate what you want to happen?	Y or N
Does the statement identify the person you will need to influence?	Y or N
Have you dated when you intend to complete each major task?	Y or N
Is the goal achievable by you within the time frame?	Y or N
Can you achieve the goal with the resources you have available to you now?	Y or N

Objective To practice setting goals by applying the ABC criteria to study skills.

Activity

1. Instruct students to select a partner. Once together, tell them they have a total of five minutes each to review and discuss their goal statements and the checklist with their partners. After 10 minutes, have partners exchange statements and rewrite the partner's goal with the information gained from their review/discussion. After five minutes, they can get back together to discuss the rewrites, ask additional goal clarifying questions and do a pair (combined effort) rewrite of each goal. Allow 10 minutes for each goal rewrite.

2. On the basis of the agreed upon final draft, partners then interview each other with the following questions. Allow five minutes for each interview.

   a. List five important steps or tasks to be accomplished that will lead to this goal.

   b. What are the major difficulties you will face?

   c. What are the "helping" forces at your disposal?

   d. How long will it take to reach your goal?

   e. What's in it for you?

Structured Discussion Conduct an all-class discussion by asking the following questions. Remember to use wait time.

Explain *achievable*, *believable* and *capable* in your own words.

Why are they called ABC's of goal setting?

Give an example of a question you might ask a person who has a goal of going to college after high school? Label it according to the ABC's and explain how it can help the goal setter?

Give an example of a question you might ask a person who has the goal of going to work after high school. Label it according to the ABC's and explain how it differs from question 3 above.

How effective are your goal-setting skills? Demonstrate or explain.

Metacognitive Processing Instruct students to do a final write-up of their study skill goals in their logs.

Follow-Up Develop other high-transfer lessons with a **Focus Activity, Activity, Structured Discussion** and **Metacognitive Processing**. For example: Have students copy or make a map of a trip across a swamp to a castle. Ask them to label the castle with a career or personal goal. Next, ask them to sketch various pitfalls and traps and to label each in reference to the goal. Discuss the importance of such a detailed plan to effectively setting goals.

Evaluation of Skills:

1. Explain each of these terms:

   achievable

   believable

   capable

2. For each of the terms above, list two questions that will appropriately help clarify a goal statement.

3. Discuss which questions you might ask yourself if you were an astronaut about to enter the space shuttle program.

4. In the past year, how have you improved as a goal setter? Give some examples.

5. In less than 75 words, construct a well-clarified goal concerning your own abilities as a goal setter.

Critical Thinking
Level III

Analyzing for Cause and Effect

Thinking Skill:

Analyzing for Cause and Effect

As the saying goes . . . Garbage In! Garbage Out!
—Anonymous

Model Lesson:

Lesson Objective To use methods for verifying cause-effect relationships.

Key Vocabulary Cause, effect, process, sequence, validity, reliability, necessary, probable, possible.

Looking Back In previous lessons, students learned the importance of setting goals as a step in identifying problems. They also learned how a problem can be defined as an obstacle or barrier to a desired goal. As a means of thinking constructively, the students learned strategies for working together in a creative climate that encouraged good thinking.

Getting Ready All around us, we see cause-and-effect relationships. When we strike a match to light a stove or start a bonfire, when we turn the key to start the car engine, when we press the switch to turn off the hall light, we see the cause-effective relationship in action. When a plane crashes, FAA investigators look for the cause. When a student is failing courses, the teachers want to discover the cause. When a machine turns out defective tools, the diemaker looks for what is causing the defect. In short, when we notice a serious problem, we cannot be satisfied with a quick fix or an instant repair. We must look for the cause of the problem.

Good thinkers do not fall into the trap of making quick fixes and instantaneous solutions; they step back, review the problem methodically, separate the problem from its *possible* causes and find data to make sure that the *necessary* cause has been found. Then, and only then, do good thinkers adjust the *necessary* cause of the problem to restore the desired effect.

For instance, if the desired effect is a well-lighted room in which you can work and read, dim lights are a problem. To discover the cause of the problem, dim lights, we have to trace the system back from the light bulbs (are they almost worn out?), across the wiring (is there a short?), to the room switch (is it working?), to the out-of-room wiring (is there a short somewhere?), to the fuse box (is anything weak?) and so forth until we pinpoint what is causing the dimness. Let's assume that we find frayed wiring going from the fuse box to the room switch. With our ohmmeter we check the flow of power on both sides of the worn wire. We note a big drop in power on the wire outside of the fray. With this data, we have verified the cause, we repair it and note that the light in the room increases at once.

As teachers who promote good thinking, we want to help students increase their skill in diagnosing the causes of increasingly more complex situations. This training helps students develop a more refined problem-solving process that doesn't lead them into the quick-fix quagmire.

Some will argue that causal analysis of a problem is a futile exercise. They tell us that it is sufficient to pick out the problem and get the solution in place as fast as possible. They cite a downed electric wire or a pothole as an example. If the wire is hanging across the highway, we know we have to fix it before someone gets electrocuted. If the hole is in the middle of a busy intersection, we have to fill it before it breaks someone's axle.

We cannot argue with such examples. Certain circumstances require that specific problems have immediate solutions. But there is danger in making the quick fix a universal approach, and we must consider it carefully. In most of the problem solving we do it is very important that we seek out the *possible* causes and then identify the *necessary* causes before we select our final solutions. To fail in this is to promote faddism and Band-Aid solutions.

There are many sophisticated examples that show the need for substantive causal analysis: airplane crashes, major epidemics, droughts, economic changes, bank failures, drug abuse, alcoholism, crime increase in specific communities, declines in academic achievement and a variety of other social and economical issues. The list can go on and on, and it well behooves us to help our students develop the skills and processes they need to thoughtfully examine each problem for its real cause(s).

At-A-Glance You will help the students get ready for this concept with a **Focus Activity** that asks students to arrange a pile of objects into a cause-effect sequence. After several groups explain their sequences, you will identify key vocabulary words in the **Lesson Objective**, check for understanding and introduce the first major task—using the fish bone to analyze possible causes. After a structured discussion and application of the concept, you will review data verification tools and provide practice tasks. Finally, you will structure transfer activities for students to apply the concepts and techniques in other subject areas.

Materials Needed

☐ Cause-effect kit for each group of five students

☐ Newsprint and tape, or easels

☐ Overhead projector and extension cord, or chalk, eraser and chalkboard

☐ Thinking Logs

Focus Activity

1. Prepare the students for a structured group task by reviewing the DOVE guidelines, the group roles and the role responsibilities. Allow the students a moment to privately review each of these in their notes and then select several different students to review them for the class. Be sure to use wait time so many of the students raise their hands for each question. Allow students from all sections of the classroom a chance to respond. Follow each student's response with positive reinforcement. If an answer is not totally correct, reinforce the correct parts and have other students add what is needed.

2. Divide the class into groups of five. Assign the group roles by identifying the person with the shortest surname in each group. Those persons are the materials managers. Rotating to the right, the other jobs in order are leader, recorder, timekeeper, observer.

3. Have each materials manager come to your desk for a kit of newsprint, markers or crayons, tape, a matchbook cover with-

out matches, one burnt match, one slightly burned piece of material and one used candle. You may vary this step by giving each group a different set of materials. For example, the sets can include a seed, a plant, a small bottle of water, a fertilizer ad or other combinations of cause-effect materials.

4. Instruct the groups to arrange their materials *by consensus* into a sequence of boxes as illustrated in the Sample Sequence Chart. Use the chalkboard or the newsprint to demonstrate. Begin with the last box; tape in it the item that represents the final result (or effect) from your represented chain of events. That might be the candle or it might be the match, or any other chosen item. Next, working backward from the final result, tell them to tape in the next box the item that was involved next (second to last) in the chain of events. Show them how to continue the process until they tape in the first box the item that was first in the chain.

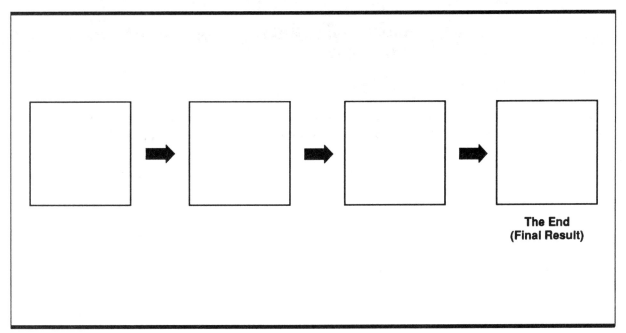

**The End
(Final Result)**

Sample Sequence Chart

All group observers should take notes as the recorders tape the objects; they will be asked to explain their groups' sequencing and reasoning. Allow five minutes for groups to tape their sequences. Let the leaders begin the activity. The timekeepers are responsible for keeping the group on track.

5. After the sequences are done, raise your hand to signal the end. Select one or more observers to describe their groups' charts and their reasoning. (If more than one group of cause-effect materials was used, be sure that all groups have a chance to share their sequences.) Ask extending questions and give positive reinforcement to each group report.

6. Summarize key elements of the reports by defining the words *cause, effect,* and the *cause and effect chain* (or sequence). Write the words on your chart and point out the examples in their models. Check for understanding by asking several students to explain each of the words in their own terms. Ask other students to give some different examples. Remember to use wait time and specific, positive reinforcement for correct answers and all good efforts.

7. End the lesson by telling the students to add the words to their vocabulary lists or logs. Instruct them to write down their explanations for the words and to include an example for each.

Activity Objective
To master a process for identifying a *highly probable* cause.

Activity
Indicate to the students that in this lesson they will not only learn how to identify causes and effects, but also how to gather data or proof that the connection or the relationship (point to the previous cause-effect chain of boxes) is faulty or damaged. They will learn some methods to track down the cause of a breakdown and to get proof that they have the right cause. For instance, they might have to show why an auto engine sputters or a brake fails. They will also be challenged to apply the skills to more abstract issues, such as a local political problem. They will learn some skills that might help them figure out the cause of a poor election turnout or why the school buses are running so late.

1. Maintaining the same groups of five from the **Focus Activity,** rotate the jobs to the right. Have the materials manager post the newsprint while the leaders review DOVE and the job responsibilities with their groups. As a class, review the steps of formal brainstorming. Check for understanding by asking students to signal thumbs up, sideways or down after your explanation. Work with the class until there is one complete explanation that eliminates all questions about what to do. Give a class "Hurrah!"

Review of Formal Brainstorming

a. Respond in turn

b. Clarify responses

c. Give pro arguments

d. Give con arguments

e. Vote on selections

---

2. Show the class a sample of a complete fish bone on an overhead or newsprint (see sample below).

Sample Fish Bone

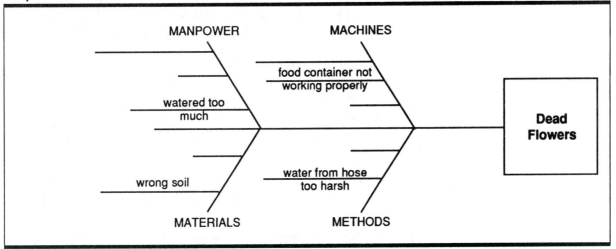

Tell the students they will be expected to complete a similar fish bone by using the first step of formal brainstorming with another cause-effective relationship.

3. Now show an empty model fish bone. On your model fish bone, label the main branches Materials, Manpower, Machines and Methods as in the following example.

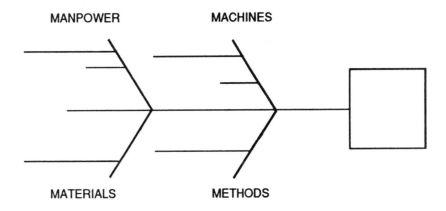

Explain to the groups that these are standard categories used in business and industry when the fish bone method of identifying *possible* causes is used. (The category headings may be altered to better fit the proposed problem.) Note that *possible* causes include all those factors that have some likelihood or good chance of having caused the problem. In selecting *possible* causes, tell the students that they are to use what knowledge and experience they have with the situation. They need to predict elements that have a reasonable chance of being the cause. They won't know yet if it's the *necessary* cause, but they are guessing. Tell the students that the four categories are there to help them expand their thoughts and look at the problem in a variety of ways.

4. Clarify the terms: **Manpower** includes the people involved in the situation who might be the *possible* cause of the problem. For instance, if a car is not running correctly, is it because the driver is abusing the car or not keeping up the maintenance schedule? **Materials** includes the "ingredients," raw materials, used in making the product and possibly the problem. For instance, is the sheet metal used in making the car of cheap quality? **Methods** includes how the product was made. For instance, is there a breakdown in the assembly line or in a way the instructions say the product is to be put together? Are the car painters using the right method to pain the car? **Machines** considers if there was something wrong with the tools used to assemble the product that caused the problem. For instance, is the robot programmed to operate correctly? Check for students' understanding of these terms.

5. Choose a problem to write in the head of the fish bone. Select four appropriate categories and then begin to model the brainstorming process. Ask a student to a) name a *possible* cause, and b) select a category to place it under. Ask a second student to do the same with a different item. The category may be the same or different. Make the entry. Ask for a third volunteer and place the entry in the category selected by the student. Check for understanding of the task. Tell students that this is the brainstorming process. When all students are clear on this process go to the next step.

6. Now prepare the groups for constructing and brainstorming their own fish bones. Instruct the recorders to construct a fish bone on their groups' newsprint. Next, on an overhead, newsprint or handout, share the Problem Topic List with the class (see list below). Have each group select one topic from the list to put in the head of the fish bone and four categories with which to label the fish bone. Then, let the groups begin their formal brainstorming—they are to think of as many possible causes of

the problem as they can. Let the groups know they have 15 minutes to complete the fish bone and to clarify their answers (using DOVE). Shorten or lengthen the limit according to the on-task time students are using in their groups. If it looks as if several groups are finishing sooner, give a shorter time line to all; if most groups seem to need more time, add five minutes.

PROBLEM TOPIC LIST

Select one of these problems for which your group can brainstorm possible solutions. Enter the key words of the problem into the head of the fish bone.

1. Paint scratches are on the driver's door of three cars fresh off the assembly line.

2. Three stores on the main street in town have broken display windows.

3. Five persons are in the hospital with serious stomach pains—all of the people ate dinner together.

4. Potholes are found on a one-year-old bridge.

5. Shirt pockets are sewn shut on all shirts mailed from the factory April 14.

6. For the third marking period in math, 75 percent of the students in one class received a D or F.

7. No TV sets are working in the school.

8. Three new tires on your dad's car have gone flat over a period of two weeks.

9. All the milk is sour on January 19 in the local grocery store.

10. Within a year's time, 46 of the 50 trees on your street die.

11. Two-thirds of the hamburgers sold in your lunchroom last week were burned.

12. Your car runs out of gas 30 miles from the nearest gas station.

13. The new record album you opened has a three-inch scratch.

14. Your new stereo is out of tune three days after you buy it.

Monitor the groups. When asked questions about the content of the problems by any group member, refer the question back to the group leader. When asked process questions, redirect the question to the group before giving your response. Encourage leaders to refer to their notes on processing for a reminder of how to structure the formal brainstorming (DOVE).

7. After 15 minutes or after all groups have finished their fish bones and clarifications, instruct the materials managers to hang a second sheet of newsprint and to create a pro-con chart. Review the steps for constructing a pro argument: Each member privately selects three items from the fish bone chart that he/ she believes are the *most* important and *probable* causes. Next, each member lists two reasons in the log for why those items are important and/or probable causes.

8. After all students have listed their top three causes and their probable criterion, have each group compile a list of its members' arguments. In turn, each group member identifies one cause he/she chose and the reason it was chosen. The recorder adds the member's item to the first column of the chart, Item, and the reasoning to the second column, Pros (see sample below).

Dead Flowers

Item	Pros	Cons
Too much water	Very possible	
	Easy with big can	
	Forget when last watered	
Bad soil	Need nitrogen	

The next person in turn says his/her reason for choosing the same item, if he/she has it written down. Each group stays with the same item until all members who chose it have given their reasons and the recorder has added those reasons to the group's list of pros. Once all the reasons are listed, the next person in turn identifies a new item from his/her list and the reason for choosing it. Again, all members contribute in turn their reasons for choosing the new item. The listing continues until all items from the private lists are posted on the master group list. Model this process for making pro arguments with one group and check for understanding of the instructions. Allow 10 minutes for groups to compile their lists of pros.

9. Once the groups have completed their lists of pro arguments, tell them they are to make a list of con arguments. For this list, instruct students to name arguments against the pro arguments *already* listed—no new items or arguments may be added. Model the procedure again, having students first list their con arguments individually and then in turn within their groups. Monitor the groups for 10 minutes or the time needed to complete the task. Allow five minutes for groups to clarify any ideas on the pro-con lists.

Dead Flowers

Item	Pros	Cons
Too much water	Very possible	Other flowers are OK
	Easy with big can	
	Forget when last watered	Dry when watering
Bad soil	Need nitrogen	

10. Next, let the groups have a few minutes to reflect on their lists. Then have each vote on its items on the *probable* cause list. The recorders tally the yes and no votes for each item. The three items with the most yes votes are the winners selected for verification. If a tie occurs, groups should rediscuss and revote on those two items—only those two items.

11. Have the group reporters present their results to the class, describe the three items their groups selected, and give the group's reasoning. After the reports are finished, have students rearrange the chairs to face the blackboard. In a semicircle, begin the class discussion with the lead-in:

> In examining for cause and effect, I learned . . . .

Wrap around the class eliciting responses until all students have given their ideas. As a follow-up question, ask for the common ideas that were shared in the wraparound. Use wait time and encourage several students to give summaries of the common responses. Let them explain how the responses were related and have them give examples. Next, ask students for other instances in their lives in which cause-effect analysis might be important to use and situations in which it would not be important.

Metacognitive Processing

Instruct students to divide a page in their logs into two columns—column 1 headed Plus and column 2 headed Minus. In column 1 have them list the advantages of doing a causal analysis; in 2 have them list the disadvantages.

CAUSAL ANALYSIS	
Plus	**Minus**

Next, ask the class to think about the steps they took to identify the probable causes. Solicit their responses and list them on the board or overhead. After you have gathered all the ideas, reduce the list to these five: (a) know the problem, (b) select identifying categories, (c) select *possible* causes by category, (d) estimate *probability*, and (e) make a final selection. Clarify each one by referencing the fish bones made in the lesson. Ask students to highlight the differences between *possible* and *probable* causes. End by instructing the students to enter the five steps for finding *probable* causes into their logs. At this point, also have students enter their new vocabulary words into their notes; ask them to include their own explanations and examples for each word.

Short Practices:

In these practices, groups of students or individuals practice the key steps in selecting highly *probable* causes and better understand the key concepts of cause-effect analysis. The first practices are for in-class work so students may receive guidance and immediate feedback on their learning. Several practices from the newspaper and news magazines reinforce the skills and initiate transfer. As students become more comfortable with the process steps, increase the difficulty of their practices with more complex articles, longer articles and at-home practices.

■ Divide the class into groups of three and review formal brainstorming, causal analysis and the fish bone process. Distribute articles from yesterday's newspaper of the past week's news magazines to each trio. Instruct the groups to apply the five steps in causal analysis to their assigned articles—(a) knowing the problem, (b) selecting identifying categories, (c) selecting *possible* causes by category, (d) estimating *probability*, (e) making a final selection.

After each group has completed its analysis, have them all (a) present their charts to the class, (b) hand in individual summaries of the process and its results, or (c) exchange charts with another group and explain what they did. After the projects are presented or turned in, conduct a structured discussion by asking students to respond to one or more of the following:

How do you think about causes and effects now as compared to before this practice and other practices?

How are you improving in your ability to analyze causes and effects?

How might you improve in this analysis?

Allow time for metacognitive processing by having students complete one of these lead-ins in their logs:

Today I learned . . . .

About causes, I wonder . . . .

About effects, I wonder . . . .

When doing cause-effect analysis, I think best when I . . . .

■ Focus students' thinking by asking volunteers to share examples from their school experiences that explain causes and effects. As a student presents an example, have the student also draw the sequence on the board. Model this example for the students: The full garbage can in the cafeteria is caused by students who empty trash into the can after eating. The trash is caused by paper wrappers on the food and empty milk cartons. Empty milk cartons are caused by . . . .

Next, assign individuals or small groups to select a problem they face when trying to complete homework assignments on time. Instruct the groups to use formal brainstorming to complete a fish bone. Ask them to share their completed fish bones and discuss with the class some of these questions:

Why is causal analysis necessary?

When would you NOT use causal analysis?

How well do you do causal analysis as a group? as an individual?

Allow time for metacognitive processing by having students do a fish bone in their logs on an academic or work problem that is challenging them. Before making the fish bones, students should jot down from memory the five steps of causal analysis that they are going to use to solve their chosen problems.

Transfer Lesson:
Current Events/ Looking Around Society

Focus Activity Display the real thing or a drawing of one or more of the following objects: a broken chair, a flat tire, a broken glass, a computer printout, a painting, a sculpture, a ceramic pot. Keep the items in two classes: damaged goods and new creations. Ask students to give reasonable guesses (ones with a high degree of probability or likelihood) about the most likely cause of the condition of the products shown. For each guess ask the student to chart out the steps of the cause-effect change they predict on the board. Ask the student to explain the basis of the causal connection he/she made—direct experience, reading, data collected, etc.

Objective To practice causal analysis skills on current social issues.

Activity

1. Identify a social issue—such as urban poverty, malnutrition, highway safety or substance abuse prevention—that is of current interest and importance. Assign one issue to the entire class or break the class into cooperative groups and assign each group a different issue. Instruct the students or groups to gather all the newspaper and news magazine stories they can over a period of two weeks on the topic assigned to them. After students have gathered their information, continue with this lesson.

2. If students are working in small groups, review DOVE, group roles and formal brainstorming on the fish bone before the class begins the next task.

3. Once students have their information and review the rules for causal analysis allow them 30 minutes to construct their cause-effect charts and perform a causal analysis on their researched issues. Check to be sure they are following the rules of formal brainstorming if they are in groups. Allow the students time to review the content of their charts and the decisions they made.

Structured Discussion When the reports are completed, put the following questions on the overhead to review the charts and the decisions made:

How probable is the cause?

What evidence from the clippings supports this probability?

What thinking did you do to arrive at this conclusion?

How solid is the causal connection?

Invite at least three students to answer each of the questions. Tell them that you intend to call on a large number of students in this discussion and that it is probable that someone who answers early will not be called on more than twice. Randomly distribute the chance to respond and avoid calling upon the same student more than twice. When needed, ask for clarification and extension of students' answers.

Metacognitive Processing Conclude this transfer lesson by having students select one article from the newspaper that describes either an achievement, a problem, an accident or a natural disaster. Review key vocabulary and provide this outline for students to construct an essay on the chosen events.

> I. In your log, provide the following information: Who is involved? What happened? What caused the event or result? (Make a small fish bone showing the *possible* causes.) What is the proof provided about the *most probable* cause?
>
> II. In your log, complete this information:
>
> Paragraph 1 Briefy describe the event and the cause you selected as most probable.
>
> Paragraph 2 Give the details of the event including who, what, when and where.
>
> Paragraph 3 Identify the likely causes.
>
> Paragraph 4 Identify the cause you selected as the most likely cause and give the reasons for your choice.
>
> Paragraph 5 Give a summary of the cause-effect relationship.
>
> III. In your log, write a rough draft of your essay. In this draft, do not worry about spelling, punctuation or other fine points. Concentrate on your word choice and the arrangement of your ideas in the sentences and the paragraphs. If you have questions, signal for my help.
>
> IV. Edit your draft. Check vocabulary, spelling, punctuation and grammar. Ask a partner to do the second edit by marking only what might be a possible mistake. Correct the mistakes. When in doubt, ask me.
>
> V. Write the final draft and hand it in as your formal essay.

Follow-Up Have students interview a senior citizen. Instruct the students to find out how the interviewees think young people are directing their lives. What directions do they see young people taking? What evidence does that person cite to support his vision? What does that person believe has caused these situations or events? Have students write up their findings and turn them in as a report. Or, allow students to share their findings with the class so that classmates can identify trends and commonalities among the interviews.

Transfer Lesson:

Causes and Effects in Science

Focus Activity Ask the students to spend a few moments privately reviewing the steps for analyzing a cause-effect relationship: (a) know the problem, (b) set categories for possible causes, (c) use the fish bone to find *possible* causes, (d) gather sufficient evidence for proof of high probability, and (e) select a *probable* cause. (Note: This does not ask the student to give final proof to establish a definite cause.) Ask several students to walk through the steps with an example. Be sure that your selection of volunteers is random and includes low performers as well as high performers. Give clues, ask for specifics and reinforce all students' answers equally. Conclude by checking for students' understanding of the key vocabulary words.

Objective To transfer cause-effect analysis skills and processes to the world of chemistry, physics, biology, earth, etc.

Activity

1. Have all students bring their science textbooks to class to read and perform the following activities or assign the following tasks as homework. Assign a chapter in the textbook and instruct students to think about cause-effect processes they come across while reading the chapter. (This lesson works particularly well when the class is studying a process such as photosynthesis or an application problem such as acid rain, soil erosion, the production of electric power, etc. It is designed to help students practice thinking about causes and effects in science.) Suggest to the students that they keep a two-column list of causes and effects in their notes as they read the chapter or have them fill in one when they are done.

TEXT CHAPTER ON GREENHOUSE EFFECT

Causes	Effects
Sun Rays	Warm Earth

2. Allow students to pick a partner with whom they have not recently worked and who has one personal quality or characteristic in common with them. Have the partners first compare their lists in search of similarities. Next, have them resolve their differences. Allow five minutes for making comparisons and five minutes for resolving differences.

3. Now, ask the pairs to construct a cause-effect fish bone that (a) identifies the major result or effect discussed in the chapter, (b) the major categories that the possible causes can be broken down into, and (c) possible causes they brainstormed. Demonstrate with the model if necessary. Allow 10 to 15 minutes for students to complete their fish bones.

4. Each pair is expected to identify evidence from the text that supports its selection of the most probable cause. Students may need five more minutes to get together their supporting evidence.

Structured Discussion Instruct each pair to match up with another pair. Have the foursomes compare and contrast their charts and their supporting evidences. After five minutes, identify groups that have any remaining disagreements. Select one or two groups to share their disagreements with the class and to present the evidence they have supporting their cases. The other students may ask clarifying questions, raise issues and point out perceived discrepancies. Encourage students to listen carefully. End each group's discussion after five minutes, identify the unresolved issues on the blackboard or overhead and then go to the next group's disagreement. During the class discussion, resolve the issues using the evidence in the text. If the issue is not resolvable in the text, solicit volunteers to find back-up evidence from sources of their choice. Students may work on this out-of-class task together or alone. Set a time line to complete out-of-class follow-up.

Metacognitive Processing Have students complete one of these lead-ins in their logs:

> About causes and effects, I wonder . . . .
>
> About causes and effects, I learned . . . .
>
> About causes and effects, I discovered . . . .

Follow-Up Choose a historical event or scientific discovery. Have students read a biographical account of a person (or persons) that were involved with that event. Structure an activity in which student groups discuss the person's (or persons') relationship to the event. What effect did the person(s) have? A contributing cause? How important? What data will support the argument?

Or, instead of a historical account, take an important and current issue facing the school or community. Pair off students and have them construct collages on that issue. The collages should show the cause-effect relationships involved in the issue.

Transfer Lesson:
History/ A Chain of Events

Focus Activity Review the five steps of the cause-effect process, the key vocabulary words and at least one example of the process in relation to historic events—for example, the French Revolution, the causes of the pilgrims leaving England and the causes of the Civil War. Next, choose material from a social studies textbook, film or supplementary readings—major events such as causes of war, emigration and exploration of a new territory work particularly well with this lesson—and assign it to students for review. The materials should describe explicitly or implicitly the causes of a certain event or chain of events. Finally, have students construct a time line of the events discussed in the assigned material.

Objective To transfer the skills and concepts of cause and effect to the study of historic events.

Activity

1. Tell the class it is now ready to investigate its time lines for possible cause-effect relationships. Invite the students to star with an asterisk (*) those events on their time lines that were

contributing causes to some other event or events on the time line. Mark the model on the board or overhead with an arrow from the starred events to the resulting event.

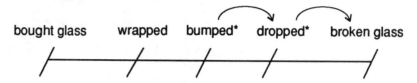

2. Now, have students identify with two stars or asterisks (**) those events which had a major effect on the final result under review. Demonstrate on the model by drawing an arrow from the double starred (**) events to the final result.

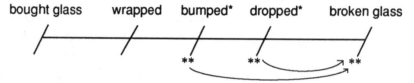

3. Divide the class into groups of threes. Identify the key roles for the group members: recorder, timekeeper, leader/materials manager. Supply each group with tape, a marker and newsprint. Before beginning the activity, review with the groups the DOVE guidelines for brainstorming and tell them they are expected to follow the guidelines throughout the activity.

4. Have students begin the group activity by making a group list of the events each member chose as a contributing factor to the final event. In turn, each student is to list an event labeled with two stars. Don't forget to allow students time to clarify each item on the list; this is an important step in formal brainstorming.

5. Briefly review the pro-con chart—how it is created and what it is for using the following chart.

REVIEW
Making a Pro-Con Chart

(1) As a group, brainstorm an unduplicated list of items.
(2) Individually, select the top three items and write two advantages (pros) for selecting each.
(3) As a group, list the items and the pro arguments each member chose.
(4) Individually, select three of the items listed and give two cons countering the pros already listed. You may not offer cons to other items unless you also offer cons to your own ideas!
(5) As a group, list each member's cons in turn.
(6) As a group, vote to select the top three items from the pro-con chart.

ITEM	PROS	CONS

Structured Discussion Select three to four groups and have them share their results and final arguments with the class. Ask clarifying questions and promote discussion after each report by asking the class to respond to these questions:

Does this group have sufficient evidence to support its argument?

If not, what more is needed?

What would happen if any one of the causes listed never occurred?

Metacognitive Processing Have each student construct in his/her log a cause-effect time line of a major event in his/her life. Instruct each student to list the sequence of events and double star the causal relationships.

Follow-up Assign students a short story or novel to read. From the story, have groups of three to five students construct a fish bone analysis of a problem one of the character's experiences. Again, the groups should use formal brainstorming and reduce their ideas down to three that they agree are the most important (using the pro-con chart). When the group analyses are complete a) have each student write a five-paragraph essay with examples from the story to argue his/her case, or b) have students write a story in which characters face problems with similar causes to the ones their groups discussed, or c) have students join with others to produce a group report of their analyses.

Evaluation of Skills:

1. Explain each of these terms:

   a. effect
   b. probable cause

2. Explain the steps in making a causal analysis.

3. Listen to this story (or another story): Once upon a time there were three little pigs. A wolf came along. Since he hadn't eaten, he was hungry. At the first house, which was made of straw, he knocked. When the pig didn't answer, he huffed and puffed until the house fell in. Because the first pig had no house, he ran next door to his brother's house. The door was locked. The wolf grabbed him and ate him up.

   a. Make a time line and place the events from the story in chronological order.

   b. Make a list of the four causal statements in the story and note their immediate effects.

   c. Identify the final effect.

4. When would a causal analysis help you? When would it not be so helpful? What might be difficult/easy in doing your analysis?

Thinking For Problem Solving Level III

Analytic Problem-Solving for Solutions

Thinking Skill:

Analytic Problem-Solving for Solutions

The message from the moon . . . is that no problem need any longer be considered insoluable.

—Norman Cousins

Model Lesson:

Lesson Objective To master the skills and processes for creatively solving problems and challenges.

Key Vocabulary Cognitive map, solution, result, outcome, creativity.

Looking Back In developing a classroom climate that promotes thinking by *all* students, teachers have introduced a variety of divergent and convergent thinking skills to their classes. Students have learned to think about goals and to identify the obstacles or problems that block them from achieving their goals. They have learned how to analyze problems for *possible* and *probable* causes, to seek proof by data and to weigh evidence with as little bias as possible. The students have practiced these skills and applied them to academic and real-life situations. They have learned to work cooperatively, to challenge fuzzy thinking and to raise important questions. Most importantly, they have learned to focus on how they think and to find ways to improve the quality of their thinking.

Getting Ready Now is the hour that most of us love: to create solutions which remedy problems, overcome roadblocks and move us directly to our goals. As we think about the solutions we desire, it is important that we remind ourselves of what promotes and hinders the creative spirit.

When students are being challenged to develop their creative thinking skills, it goes without saying that we must free them from classroom practices which inhibit their ability to stretch their minds into new and adventurous ideas. Adolescents, by the nature of their age, are torn between their desire to conform in all ways of thinking and acting with their peers, and the desire to be unique and creative individuals. If they are to grow into mature and constructive problem-solvers, it is important that we help them survive the restrictions of their age and develop the creativity that is inherent in each of them.

The starting point is our value system. Do we place sufficient importance on higher-level thinking? In our classrooms, do we behave in such a way as to encourage inventiveness, reward fresh insights, reinforce initiative and praise experimentation of ideas? Or do we invite imitations, reward conformity, reinforce routine responses and praise the nondescript?

Students learn quickly what is expected of them. If we make the classroom a haven for the minimal, we will quickly see many students resting in that safe harbor. On the other hand, if we make the classroom an adventurous sea of thought, we will see students accepting the challenges of the wildest storms, struggling with ideas and finding new and better ways to sail the waters.

Working successfully with students whose minds are dulled by TV requires a skilled and subtle teacher who knows the power of high expectations. The effective teacher assiduously avoids the killer classroom behaviors that so readily deter students' creative thinking and turns them into positive, nurturing actions (see the following chart below).

HOW TO NURTURE CREATIVE THINKING

- Allow for a variety of thinking strategies.
- Accept "imperfect" and different projects.
- Expect all students—perfect, imperfect, awkward or whatever—to be themselves.
- Keep competition in its place and inspect each student's quantity and quality of work on an individual basis.
- Give unconventional qualities of a creative project *at least* as students a much weight as the conforming aspects.
- Build enough time into your lessons, discussions etc. for *all* students—the slower ones and the faster ones—to think.
- Emphasize the thinking processes that go into making/performing each final project.
- Make a point to support students' ideas with specific, clear and obvious praise.
- Model creative and critical thinking at every chance—ask wild, unique and inspiring questions.
- Work at giving *all* students special attention—they are *all* star students and star thinkers.

Obviously, a preliminary step in promoting creative thinking is asking questions that encourage all students to predict, design, compose and solve challenging problems. Beyond that, the skilled teacher plans lessons that develop students' creative thinking skills, helps the students apply those skills to real-life situations, and at all times, supports students who produce new insights, make new discoveries and create new answers to old and nagging questions.

If we are to help our young meet the intellectual challenges of the next century, we cannot afford to accept passive learning of filtered facts as the criterion by which we measure education. If school people are to make any worthy contribution to the future, we must, as Rollow May argues, give greater priority to the development of the child's original thinking and problem solving, and a lesser priority to trouble-free obedience and attention by conformity. May wants to see teachers praise students who ask the surprising questions rather than be irritated by them; he wants teachers to favor challenging questions rather than popular answers; and he hopes there will be far fewer bright students dropping out of school than is the current case. Most of all, though, he wants to see young students learning to fight the feelings of apathy and despair that are promulgated by the powerlessness to think and create.

There are some who have a locked mind set that dealing with problems is a negative approach. This is a limiting view. Problem solving in the context used in these lessons is focused on positive achievement, conceptual growth and an increased valuing of the strength of the mind as the one great resource that gives us the opportunity to achieve our greatest successes as a human being. Each of us learns to clarify the goals that have the most meaning to us. In that process, we indeed experience obstacles and barriers that can keep us from achieving our goals. Do we ignore these? Do we quit? Or do we use that unique human quality, our thinking power, to overcome the obstacles and the problems that challenge us, and move on to accomplishing our goals, finding solutions that do the job?

Let's take some examples. A young student discovers that she has a great math talent. Early in her high school years she sets a goal to achieve a Ph.D. in math. By the end of her junior year, she has completed all the math courses offered in her high school. What can she do her senior year? The gap is a problem. It could hinder her progress toward her goal. Careful and creative thinking tells her there are many options. One is that she misses a year of math. Another is that she takes an independent study course. A third is that she takes a class at a local college. What are the advantages and disadvantages of each option?.. and so her thinking continues until she makes the final choice. She eliminates the problem and learns once again that by using her thinking skills, she can manage her life in a positive, goal-directed way.

Contrast this first example with another one. A sophomore student with special athletic skills had a goal to make the varsity basketball team. One Friday night he dropped in on a party with some friends. Beer was being served. At first thought, he remembered that the athletic code banned all drinking even in the off season. Pressure from his friends, however, soon had him drinking the beer. He rationalized with himself that there was no way he would get caught. He didn't consider any other options. The following Monday the stories were all over school—Tom got "wasted" at the party. The coach heard and let Tom know that he was ineligible for the team. The goal was there, but no thinking about solutions to the problem was there— Tom was left without a chance for achieving his goal.

Students who develop their thinking skills in the safe confines of the classroom, can refine their skills and their confidence before using them in situations outside of the classroom. As good thinkers, they learn to set goals for a positive direction in life, identify the problems that block the paths to their goals and develop creative and carefully examined solutions to their problems. They discover what they can achieve. The poor thinkers who are muddled about goals, problems and solutions see only that they are the victims of circumstance. To them, factors and people beyond their control are to be blamed for what they have failed to achieve; and there is little value in taking personal responsibility to use their thinking skills to achieve even the most minimal goals.

At-A-Glance In the **Focus Activity** for this lesson, students will conduct a treasure hunt. The students will go in search of other people in the classroom who have used their creative talents in different ways. In the lesson, students will learn to use the cognitive map as a way of webbing the attributes of creative thinking. Finally, they will learn some techniques to design a solution to a problem by synthesizing the best thinking into a creative plan.

Focus Activity

1. Invite students to review DOVE and to discuss why the guidelines are especially important in the creative thinking process.

2. Hand out a copy of the Creative People Search. Review the instructions on the copy.

3. Allow approximately five minutes for the class to perform the Creative People Search.

Materials Needed

- ☐ Handouts of the Creative People Search

- ☐ Overhead projector, extension cord, marker or blackboard chalk, and eraser

- ☐ Magazines, scissors, glue and 8" x 11" cardboard for each trio

- ☐ Problem-Solving Sequence (Transparency)

- ☐ Problem Scenarios (handout)

- ☐ Newsprint, tape and markers

- ☐ Thinking Logs

THE CREATIVE PEOPLE SEARCH:
A TREASURE HUNT

1. Fill in each box with a signature.

2. No more than one signature by a person on your sheet.

3. This will take about five minutes. Sit down when your sheet is full.

FIND SOMEONE WHO...

baked a cake	won a prize	found a lost key
_____	_____	_____

painted a picture	stopped a fight	likes to experiment
_____	_____	_____

wrote a song or poem	invented _____	is a dreamer
_____	_____	_____

has a good imagination	likes to solve math problems	hates canned TV shows
_____	_____	_____

4. Note that the people search covered a lot of ground. Have each student think about one of the statements on the Creative People Search. Have students relate their statements to what they understand creative thinking to be.

5. Use a classroom wraparound, allowing students to make a connection or to pass. On the chalkboard or overhead, draw a cognitive map. As each student gives an idea, plug it into the map. When the last student is finished, put the phrase *creative thinking* into the center of the map.

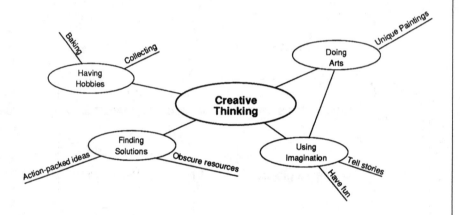

6. Give positive feedback to the students for their observation of DOVE, their contributions and their divergent thoughts. The result is the cognitive map, which identifies the critical attributes of *creative thinking*. You may wish to add a few attributes (the main offshoots), and secondary qualities (the side branches).

7. Conclude by instructing students to complete the following lead-in in their logs:

Creative thinking is . . . .

Activity Objective To master the skills and processes helpful in creatively solving problems and challenges.

Activity:

1. Tell students to form groups of three. Identify the person with the shortest hair in each group to be the leader. The leader appoints the materials manager and timekeeper, and reviews the DOVE guidelines for formal brainstorming with his/her group. Have the materials managers pick up the following: two to three magazines, a piece of 8" x 11" poster board, glue and scissors.

2. Next, have each group look through the magazines and randomly select six objects—a car, a wrench, a toothbrush, etc.—that appear to have little in common. Tell them they have five minutes to choose and cut out their items. When they are done, they are to use the six cut-outs to invent a picture of a new object that has a practical use. The groups may cut, trim and glue the pictures together to create their visions of the new objects. When the groups are done creating, allow them time to name their inventions and to post their pictures in the room.

3. Discuss with the class which attributes of creative thinking they used to create their new objects. List the attributes on the board. Encourage all students to contribute. After the list is exhausted, tell students they can use these same attributes to solve problems. Review the problem-solving sequence on the overhead:

PROBLEM-SOLVING SEQUENCE

    a. the goal
    b. the problem
    c. the cause
    d. the solution

---

4. Give copies of the Problem Scenarios handout to the class. Have each student select one of the problem scenarios. After a few minutes, instruct each student to find three other persons who have selected the same scenario.

THE PROBLEM SCENARIOS

I. Mary and Sue grew up together and have been close friends for more than a dozen years. For the past two years, Barry and Sue have dated regularly. Barry has taken a sudden, heavy interest in Mary and wants her to go to the Homecoming Dance with him. Mary keeps putting him off, but really wants to go to the dance.

II. Al likes his job stacking groceries at the local market. He has held the job for three years. He's using one-half of his weekly check to buy a used car. Because business has been so good, the manager has hired another stock boy. The manager is paying the new employee, his nephew, 20 cents more per hour than he is paying Al.

III. Rich is a straight-A student. He hopes to go to college to study premed. He has two older sisters who are already in college. His family cannot afford another full tuition and Rich is concerned that if he takes a job, his grades will suffer and hurt is chances of getting into a good premed school.

5. Have each foursome identify the person who had the most hours of sleep the previous night. That person is the leader. Instruct the leader to identify the recorder, the materials manager and the timekeeper/observer. Give them a few moments to review the role responsibilities and DOVE before handing out the newsprint, markers and tape to each materials manager.

6. Tell the groups they have three minutes to brainstorm questions they want to ask about their scenarios. After the time is up, allow three more minutes for the groups to select the three most important questions they will ask. Begin with the first scenario. Allow each group using the first scenario to ask you one question at a time. No duplications. Once all of these groups have asked their top three questions, go to the second and then the third scenario. When answering the questions, be creative. The students will have to live with the details they are given. For instance, about scenario one, students might ask, "Are theses the only people involved?" The answer can be yes or some other characters can be added—be creative but not complicated.

7. For the next five minutes, have each group of students agree upon and record responses to the following questions:

In your scenario, what is the principle character's goal?

What is the problem?

What is the cause of the problem?

Have them discuss their responses with the entire class. Reinforce their good thinking.

8. Now instruct the groups to draw their own cognitive maps. Demonstrate on the board or overhead. Have each recorder write the cause of his/her group's problem in the center of the map. Instruct the group members to generate possible solutions for the cause of the problem—remind them to offer ideas in turn, without interrupting. The person who adds an item designates whether or not the solution is a basic (main offshoot) or a refining/supportive solution (secondary branch), and determines where the idea is placed on the map.

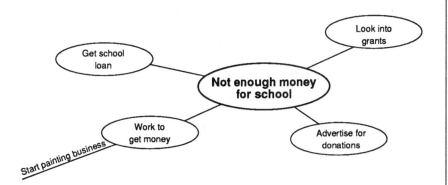

Allow eight to ten minutes for groups to map their ideas. After the maps are done, allow the groups five more minutes for clarifying their solutions and writing their clarifications on the maps.

9. Instruct the recorders to make a second chart, a pro-con chart. Review the steps in making a pro-con chart (see following review) and then allow students time to construct their arguments.

REVIEW
Making a Pro-Con Chart

(1) As a group, brainstorm an unduplicated list of items.

(2) Individually, select the top three items and write two advantages (pros) for selecting each.

(3) As a group, list the items and the pro arguments each member chose.

(4) Individually, select three of the items listed and give two cons countering the pros already listed. You may not offer cons to other items unless you also offer cons to your own ideas!

(5) As a group, list each member's cons in turn.

(6) As a group, vote to select the top three items from the pro-con chart.

ITEM	PROS	CONS

10. After the pros and cons are listed for various items, ask the leaders to take their groups through a weighed voting. Having carefully considered all arguments, each person can make three votes: a three-pointer vote for the best solution, a two-pointer for the second best and a one-pointer for the third best. The recorder tallies the votes on the newsprint. The item with the most votes wins.

11. Instruct each group to prepare a short enactment of the solution its members selected. Allow five minutes for preparation and then call upon each group to make its presentation. Each member must have some stage role (actor, narrator, etc.). Each group must present even if it is using the same scenario as another group. After each enactment, the performing group must use its newsprint to show how and why it made the solution it did.

12. Ask the class three of the following questions. Remember to use wait time, equal distribution of questions, cuing and encouragement. Seek multiple responses and give specific feedback about the quality of thinking used in the discussion.

What steps are used to arrive at a single solution?

Which of the steps was/were easiest for you? most difficult? Explain.

Why is it important to argue cons to your own pros?

When might you use a cognitive map? Give specific instances and walk us through the thinking steps you would use—topic, major ideas, details, grouping for selection, etc.

What are the advantages of using a cognitive map for you?

Metacognitive Processing Conduct an open-class brainstorming session of specific instances (begin with suggestions from above) in which someone might make a cognitive map. List the ideas on the chalkboard. After enough have been provided, instruct each student to select a topic and construct a cognitive map on that topic in his/her log. Alow three to five minutes.

Short Practices:

Continue to reinforce the creative thinking process by helping students become more adept with their cognitive maps. Encourage them to stretch their thinking, to break self-imposed restrictions on the goodness, acceptability or rightness of ideas and to seek out new combinations, different perspectives and unique arrangements.

■ To practice using the cognitive map as a creative thinking strategy, use the following planning activity. Students can use this approach for special assignments in science, social studies, English, art, health or for major tasks they want to complete in student activities, community work or career planning. Tell the students they are going to learn how to make a planning map for projects they have to complete.

On the overhead, walk students through a model project; use the Project Planning Worksheet (see following sample) and a cognitive map.

PROJECT PLANNING WORKSHEET

Date:
Proposed Ending Date:
Activity Description:

Purpose of Activity:

Desired Outcome of Activity:

Order	Key Activities	Due Dates

First, complete the basic information on the worksheet—date, proposed ending date and description of a selected project, including its purpose and the desired outcome. For example, select a project such as *choosing a college* or *getting a job*. Next, write the purpose of the project—*to get a degree in veterinary medicine* or *to save money for college*. Finally, write down the desired outcome of the project—*to own my own vet hospital* or *to get a degree in business*.

Now, show students how to map their projects. First, put the project topic in the center of the cognitive planning map. Invite the class to suggest branches and stems for you to add to the map. Make the entries on the model. For example:

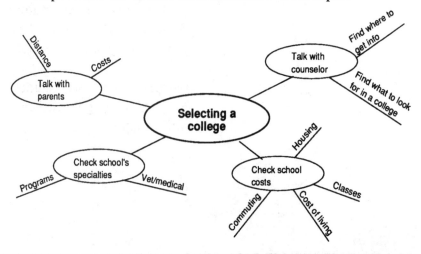

After the model is started and partially complete, show the students how to list the key activities from the map onto the worksheet. Demonstrate how to sequence the tasks and add the expected completion dates for each activity. Check for understanding.

Ask each student to choose a project to map. Once all students have chosen a project, allow 20 minutes for each individual to work on a map and worksheet alone. Walk around the classroom. Give feedback and encouragement, and offer help if asked.

Next, conduct a structured discussion for this lesson. Instruct students to select partners. Tell them each student has five minutes to walk his partner through this cognitive map. (Tell them you will announce the time.) When listening, each partner is to identify and record the strong points of the speaker's plan and to note what might be improved.

When all students have had the chance to present their plans, ask the class the following questions. Seek several responses to each.

What do you like about your plan?

How did the map help you?

Predict your chances of completing this plan.

Next, have students think about their thinking by asking them to complete one of the following lead-ins in their logs:

In my plan, I was most pleased that I . . . .

In thinking about my plan, I learned that I . . . .

I intend . . . .

■ To practice use of the cognitive map as a thought organizer, use the following short practice for taking notes—the number of practices with print, film, TV and lectures is limitless. Explain to students that the cognitive map not only helps us stretch our thinking, but also it helps us recognize patterns as an alternative to organizing lecture notes. Let the students know that using this tool as an organizer may feel awkward, but they should learn it well so that they can make an informed choice about which note-taking method—the cognitive map or the outline—

is more helpful to them. The choice is a matter of preference, usually depending on each student's style of thinking.

Distribute copies of a news article to the students. Instruct all students to read the article and pick out the key points. After they have read the article, have the students form groups of four with a leader, recorder, materials manager and timekeeper.

If necessary, ask a student volunteer from the back of the room to review on the chalkboard the use of a cognitive map. Check the class for understanding. Then, have each group make a map and enter the title of the article into the core of the map. Have the leader of each group begin the brainstorming for the map. After five to ten minutes, have several group leaders report on their groups' completed maps. Ask extending questions and give hurrahs.

Conduct a structured discussion with the class using the following questions. Solicit multiple responses, clarify and give reinforcement to each student's good thinking.

In your own words, explain a cognitive map.

List the steps in thinking through a cognitive map.

How does a cognitive map help you as a thinker?

What are some instances in which you might complete a map?

How is cognitive mapping different from outlining?

What if you were a scientist challenged to find a mysterious disease that was making everyone sick in your neighbor hood, how would you use the map?

Allow students time to reflect on this activity and their thinking by inviting them to find a story tonight in their newspaper or on the evening news. Tell them to make a cognitive map in their logs of what they read or see in the news. If time allows the next day, let students share their findings with the rest of the class.

SAMPLE ARTICLE

VIRAL MAP

First step to a cure for colds

In their frustratingly slow effort to conquer the common cold, medical scientists decades ago learned that the world's most prevalent disorder is usually caused by any of a hundred or so different kinds of viruses. Under an electron microscope, they all look like simple fuzzy balls, but the precise architecture of these so-called rhinoviruses has remained obscure. Last week, teams of scientists from Purdue and the University of Wisconsin, Madison, reported in the journal *Nature* that they had mapped in exquisite atomic detail the structure of a human cold virus called HRV14. Their achievement marked the first time that the shape of an animal virus had been so precisely determined, and raised hopes that a cure for the common cold might be possible after all.

HRV14 is marvelously complex; its genetic material is surrounded by a 20-sided outer shell that vaguely resembles a soccer ball. The sides consist of three identical triangles, each containing three proteins on its irregular surface and one below it. On the surface proteins, the researchers discovered that the features which resemble mountaintops are actually antigens, structures that antibodies seek out and attach themselves to when attacking the virus. A "canyon" snakes between these mountaintops and is believed by scientists to be shaped specifically to fit over projections, or receptors, on the surface of human cells. The virus may use this canyon to attach itself to a receptor, as a keyhole receives a key, before attacking the cell.

Armed with this knowledge of the viral topography, scientists, at least in theory, can begin closing in on a cure for the common cold. For example, a lab-made antibody designed to slide into the canyon and block it would prevent the virus from attaching to a cell. One problem with that approach, researchers say, is that antibodies are too large to enter the canyons. But another approach is possible, involving the key (the receptor) instead of the lock (the canyon). By developing a drug that somehow coats the receptors, scientists may prevent the virus from joining the cell.

In fathoming the shape of HRV14, the Purdue and Wisconsin teams depended heavily on high technology. Using X-rays produced by Cornell University's High Energy Synchrotron Source, they passed a beam through crystallized samples of the virus. Data derived from the interactions between the X-rays and the viral atomic structure were then fed into Purdue's Cyber 205 super computer, which enabled the researchers to produce a detailed three-dimensional picture of the virus. In fact, the super computer was the hero of the project. "The final set of calculations were made in a month," said Michael Rossmann, who headed the Purdue team. Without the Cyber, "They might have taken 10 years."

Transfer Lesson:

Adventures With Literature

Focus Activity   Conduct an all-class discussion about forming opinions of people and things. Are students' judgments usually correct or incorrect? How have their judgments affected their relationships with other people? Ask several students to explain how they form their impressions about people. How are those strategies similar? different? What does it take to change an opinion? How closely do students look for clues to form their opinions? Bring out discussion about predictions and how students make predictions from their judgments.

Objective   To use the cognitive map as a technique for exploring the character of each family member in the play "Death of a Salesman."

Activity   This transfer lesson uses a drama, but you can easily adapt it to a short story, novel, nonfiction or biography. Furthermore, although this sample focuses on character study, you can create other lessons that focus on theme, style, setting, etc.

1. Draw a cognitive map on the overhead or chalkboard. Write the names of the five family members from Miller's play "Death of a Salesman,"on the five major offshoots. As the students read each act of the play, they are to make offshoots listing clues to each person's character. Instruct the students to note how the characters act toward each other, what they do or say, what emotions are suggested, etc. The class will review the cognitive maps at the end of each act.

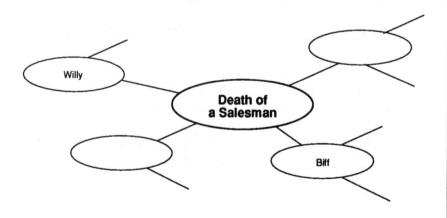

2. At the end of the first act, assign students to groups of three. In the groups, they will compare their maps and agree on changes in the basic branches. After 10 minutes, call for some sample reports on each character. After each character report, ask the following: On the basis of what you know so far, what can you predict about the character's reaction under family stress? What suggests that your prediction is solid? Seek several points of view and push for evidence from the text. Always check to see who in the class disagrees and why. Give hurrahs for complete thinking.

3. At the end of the second act, have students join in new groups of three, not the same students who worked together after the first act. Once again they should compare the branches and agree on changes. Ask each group to identify what the second act brought out that reinforced predictions made in the last discussion and what was new or different. Will anyone change their first prediction and why? Obtain several points of view, push for evidence and give specific feedback for good thinking.

4. At the end of each succeeding act, form new groups with different members. Compare branches and agree on changes. Check out the previous predictions for their accuracy.

Structured Discussion At the end of the play and after the final maps are finished, discuss the following questions:

Which character reacted in the end as predicted in the first act?

Which did not? Why not?

Given the evidence charted on the maps, can you identify inconsistent behaviors by any of the characters?

What if Biff were your son? How would you have treated him differently than his father did? What if Willy were your father? How would you have treated him differently than his sons did?

What are the moral lessons someone can learn from this play?

Metacognitive Processing Ask students to take out their logs and write a brief letter to a person they think should read this play. Be sure students explain why they think that person should read it. Allow five to eight minutes for this activity.

Follow-Up Have students track their interactions with other people for a week—tracking what each person does verbally and nonverbally. At the end of the week have students reread their notes as if they were reading about other people or characters in a story. Review the cognitive map and then give them time to map their interactions. What patterns do they see in the actions and reactions of the characters? Could any of the results or reactions been predicted?

Allow students time to reflect upon the interactions in their journals. Ask them to predict what their interactions might tend to be in the future. What might be done differently? How might their new overviews affect how they see others' actions? How can they use these insights to solve problems or better yet, prepare or prevent problems from happening in the future?

Transfer Lesson:

Looking Into History/ The Great Depression

Focus Activity Review DOVE and the responsibilities of each group role with the class. Ask for explanations and examples of *goal, problem, cause* and *solution*.

Objective To practice divergent thinking in exploring possible solutions to the causes of the Great Depression.

Activity

1. Assign students the textbook chapter on the Great Depression (or adapt this lesson to other historic content.) Instruct them to individually prepare a time line of the major events that led up to Black Friday.

2. Make a class time line on the chalkboard. Have students fill in the events.

3. Ask students to identify the problems of Black Friday and the Great Depression as faced by each of the following:

   the president of the United States
   a bank president
   a bank depositor
   a stock broker

4. After discussing the possible problems, select one serious problem for each of the characters listed. Group students into threes with a leader, a recorder and materials manager/time-keeper. Have the groups select one character/problem from the list and create a 100-word scenario about the character. Tell the groups to list the high points of the scenario on newsprint. Each scenario should focus on a character's problem as caused by the collapse of the market.

5. After the scenarios are listed, ask each group to exchange its scenario with another group. The new group may ask the originator group no more than 10 "fill-in" questions about the scenario. With the given information, new group should construct a cognitive map to identify alternative solutions to the problem.

6. Instruct the originator groups to get their original scenarios back with their new maps of possible solutions. Have the originators construct pro-con charts to guide the discussion of all their optio

7. On the basis of the pro-con chart, each originator group should select the solution it agrees is the best. Have the groups present their cases to the class.

Structured Discussion
Invite the entire class to respond to the following questions:

For your group's solution, forecast the consequences of its implementation.

How would you test the validity of your solution?

Formulate a theory about the best ways to avoid a repeat of the same collapse.

Seek a variety of responses for each question, press for clarification and supporting reasons to the ideas. Reinforce complete thinking.

Metacognitive Processing
In his/her log, have each student write an editorial for the local paper. Tell them, "As editor, you see some of the same trends that led to the Great Depression being repeated by the local bank. Present your preventative solutions." Tell them they will have 10 minutes to complete their editorials.

Follow-Up
Have students pick an issue currently facing their neighborhood, community or state (or assign one topic to the entire class). Allow them time to research their topics; they can attend a local town or board meeting, talk to neighbors and members of the community, read the paper, magazines or newsletters. Have each student make a cognitive map on the issue, including the facts as well as the conflicting arguments. Let them continue to solve the problems using their cognitive maps and pro-con charts. Allow time for students to share their problems and solutions as a class.

Transfer Lesson:

Solving Environmental Issues in Science

Focus Activity Read the following letter to the class (or adapt this lesson to another science-related issue in the community, state or country).

Dear Dad and Mom,

How are you? Things are fine here in the New York mountains. We have our field station on the side of Whiteface Mountain. We are about a 20-minute ride from Lake Placid. Next weekend, a bunch of us are going to Placid to tour the Olympic sites. They won't be the same in the summer, but it will be something to do.

The people on the project are very nice. My roommate is from Princeton. There are several grad students from SUNY, Albany. The project is run out of Harvard. I am the youngest person here. Everyone except myself and the SUNY people has a Ph.D. in one research science or another.

Don't laugh when I tell you what we do. Every morning I have to go to a station at the tip of the mountain and gather clouds. That's what I said. We have big plastic bags that scoop up the moisture. We bring the moisture back here and then we run it through machines that analyze its acid content. Other people gather soil samples and rain samples for the same thing. The disappointing part is that we can analyze the cloud water and the earth water and we know how certain amounts of acidity are killing the spruce, but we are 10 years away from having the technology that will prove whether the rain and clouds are delivering enough to meet the guidelines for cause and effect. So it will all stay as "theory." OOPS. It's almost time to go and collect the clouds. I will have to sign off now.

Love to all,
Your Loving Daughter

Tell the students that in our high-tech world there are many environmental problems. There is also much disagreement about the seriousness of the problems and how to solve them. One of the serious problems about which there is much disagreement is acid rain. In this lesson, tell students they are going to have a chance to investigate the problem of acid rain and to develop some creative solutions.

Objective To use creative thinking in developing possible solutions to a critical environmental issue.

Activity

1. Select one of the films available about the acid rain problem. Prepare the students for viewing the film. Tell them that they will be asked to make a cognitive map of the ideas in the film as soon as the showing is over. Remind them that the maps will require them to identify the problem and then brainstorm solutions. Show the film.

2. After the film, divide the class into groups of four. Assign the person in each group with a birthday closest to the end of year as the timekeeper. That person assigns the leader, the recorder and the materials manager. Review DOVE and the responsibilities of each role. Give newsprint, tape and markers to the materials managers.

3. Hold an all-class brainstorming session of the problems identified in the film and make a master list of them on the board. Instruct each group to select one of the problems for use in its cognitive map. Tell the groups they will have 10 minutes to brainstorm solutions on their maps.

4. At the end of the time, have each group select the element from its map that it wants to design into a formal presentation for the class. Tell them their solutions will be judged on the following criteria: imagination, cost-effectiveness and solid rationale. In its presentation, each group should outline (a) its goal, (b) the major ingredients in the package, (c) the resources available, (d) the benefits, (e) a time line, and (f) cost estimates. If a group does not have sufficient data from the film, it may have the chance to use other reference materials. All members must participate in the presentations. Visuals are encouraged.

Structured Discussion After the last presentation, ask the class by a show of hands to evaluate each of the proposals. Students do not evaluate their own group's work. On a scale of 1(low) to 5(high) have students rate each proposal for (a) imagination, (b) cost-effectiveness, and (c) solid rationale. The group recorders mark the score of each. After the scores are complete, ask individuals to explain their evaluations.

Metacognitive Processing In their logs, have students complete one of these lead-ins:

> I wonder . . . .
>
> I predict . . . .
>
> What if . . . ?

Follow-Up Suppose the earth's ozone layer opened up completely? Suppose we went to war with Canada using chemical warfare? Suppose we let so many industries and people pollute our air that it became humanly unbearable? Suppose one of the science-related problems our society is facing now is not fixed in time, how will we deal with the consequences? Take a problem and brainstorm with the class possible and probable outcomes that could result if that problem is not confronted. From the brainstormed list on the board, ask students to form small groups and brainstorm solutions to the consequences. Using pro-con charts, the groups should develop supporting evidences and arguments to present to the class.

Evaluation of Skills:

1. List human characteristics that seem to indicate creative thinking. For each example, name a well-known person who exhibits that characteristic and justify your choice.

2. Elaborate on this cognitive map of the problem-solving process.

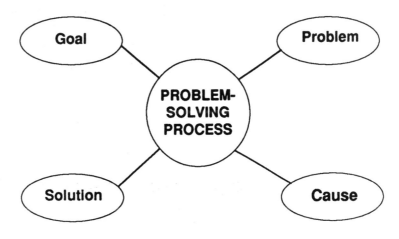

3. Write a brief expository statement about cognitive mapping. Include possible applications and pros and cons of the maps.

Keep Them Thinking Level III

Masters Appendix

Premise 1

The teacher is the architect of the intellect.

A teacher affects eternity. He never knows where his influence ends.
—Henry Adams

Premise 2

The student is the capable apprentice.

'Come to the edge,' he said.
They said, 'We are afraid.'
'Come to the edge,' he said. They came.
He pushed them . . . and they flew.
—Apollinaire

Premise 3

Thinking is more basic than the basics— it frames all learning.

Intelligent behavior is knowing what to do when you don't know what to do.
—Arthur Costa

ABC's Of Goal Setting

Realistic problem-solving begins with the A, B and C of goal setting. They are the criteria that can help students measure the quality of their goals.

Achievable: An achievable goal is one that the individual can trace, step by step, from his/ her current place to the actual attainment—the goal is clear and explicit. On the long climb to the goal, the individual knows each step in sequence, which steps are critical and which steps may need some adjusting. For instance, Sue, an outstanding 15-year-old tennis player, wants to reach her goal—to play professional tennis. She has thought carefully about what she must do. She knows, for instance, that she must practice a minimum of four hours per day, continue her weight program, control her diet as prescribed by the team nutritionist, strengthen her serve, and so on. By breaking her long-range goal into manageable, sequenced steps, she makes her goal more *achievable*.

Believable: A believable goal is one which is built on a careful assessment of what is within our grasp. All students need to use their personal experiences to refine their visions of what is possible or what is within their grasp. Direct experience can be the best teacher; indirect experience also helps. For instance, Sue may wish to be a professional tennis player, but for Sue's mother, that goal is not very believable. Sue's mother has never read about, saw on TV or at the movies nor heard about a woman becoming a pro tennis player. The dream is virtually *unbelievable* because she hasn't seen any concrete models. Sue, however, has read about women pros in *Sports Illustrated*, seen women's tennis at Wimbelton, attended a pro tournament at Forest Hills, got Steffi Graf's autograph, and interviewed her next-door neighbor, a pro women's tennis coach, for the high school paper. Sue's first-hand contact with women pros makes her goal *believable*.

Capable: A capable goal is one built on solid assessment of one's strengths and weaknesses. The assessment is solid to the degree that good evidence from reliable sources is available to tell students what they can and cannot do. Sue's coach is a reliable source. Every week she previews a videotape of Sue's practices. Together they keep a tally of how well Sue does with each type of shot. They measure her strengths, accuracy and attention. They can compare her skills to others in her ability class as well as to women pros to evaluate her *capability*.

The ABC's of goal setting help students clarify their goals and bring them into a line that is more realistic. When taken together, the ABC's help students form a more realistic, intertwined picture of what is desired and the best means to that goal.

Newspaper Basketball Rules

I.   Everyone gets a partner. The two of them are a team. Each team, one at a time, makes three throws. One partner throws and the other one retrieves. Three throws comprise a team's round.

II. The only way to score points during the rounds is by throwing the newspaper basketball into the waste can. The score for each "basket" is determined by the line from which a player throws it.

III. Before starting a round, each team predicts what its final score for the round will be. Each team must write down and announce its predicted score to the class. In addition, each team must announce which lines it will attempt its three throws from to reach its predicted score.

IV. Teams may attempt to make all throws from behind one line or from a variety of lines. Each team is responsible for keeping its own working score during its round.

V.   At the end of a round, the team's score is recorded on the official score sheet. After all teams have had a round, the team with the highest score wins. Play-off rounds may be necessary to break first-place ties.

Types Of Goals

- ❏ a career goal
- ❏ a skill goal
- ❏ an academic achievement goal
- ❏ a product goal
- ❏ a task goal
- ❏ a personal relationship goal
- ❏ a personal improvement goal
- ❏ a family goal
- ❏ a spiritual goal
- ❏ a physical achievement goal
- ❏ a travel goal

Goal Clarifying Questions

A = Achievable

What are the steps you will have to take to accomplish this goal?
Can you sequence them?
Which are the three most critical steps? Why?
Which are the least important?
Which steps may need some adjusting? Which will cause you to adjust your
    own ideals, beliefs, habits or lifestyle?
How ready are you to make adjustments to reach your goal?
What will you not change or give up?
What are the major external blocks in your path?
How will you handle these?
What resources do you have that can help you? How will you use them?
What is the major hurdle? Which resource will help the most in overcoming
    that hurdle?

B = Believable

What experiences have you had that will help you achieve your goal?
Which are most critical? How will they help?
What models do you have in thinking you can reach this goal?
What tangible evidence will you have to tell you that you are successful?
What means do you have to critique your progress, give feedback and check
    your assumptions about yourself?

C = Capable

What personal strengths do you have that will help you achieve your goal?
What are the limits within yourself that will hinder you?
How do you plan to deal with your limits? Use your strengths?
What alternatives have you considered? Are any possible?
Can you influence persons who can assist you? What do you intend to do?

DOVE Rules for Brainstorming

Defer judgment—accept all ideas, list everything, evaluate later

Opt for original and off-beat—anything goes, especially different and crazy ideas

Vast numbers of ideas are best—get many ideas, the more the better

Expand by association—piggyback off of each other's ideas

Goal Clarifying Checklist

Y   or   N

Does your statement indicate what
you want to happen?
☐   ☐

Does the statement identify the
person you will need to influence?
☐   ☐

Have you dated when you intend to
complete each major task?
☐   ☐

Is the goal achievable by you within
the time frame?
☐   ☐

Can you achieve the goal with the
resources you have available to you
now?
☐   ☐

Evaluation of Skills: Scoring Goals!

1. Explain each of these terms:

   achievable

   believable

   capable

2. For each of the terms above, list two questions that will appropriately help clarify a goal statement.

3. Discuss which questions you might ask yourself if you were an astronaut about to enter the space shuttle program.

4. In the past year, how have you improved as a goal setter? Give some examples.

5. In less than 75 words, construct a well-clarified goal concerning your own abilities as a goal setter.

Problem Topic List

Select one of these problems for which your group can brainstorm possible solutions. Enter the key words of the problem into the head of the fish bone.

1. Paint scratches are on the driver's door of three cars fresh off the assembly line.

2. Three stories on the main street in town have broken display windows.

3. Five persons are in the hospital with serious stomach pains—all of the people ate dinner together.

4. Potholes are found on a one-year-old bridge.

5. Shirt pockets are sewn shut on all shirts mailed from the factory April 14.

6. For the third marking period in math, 75 percent of the students in one class received a D or F.

7. No TV sets are working in the school.

8. Three new tires on your dad's car have gone flat over a period of two weeks.

9. All the milk is sour on January 19 in the local grocery store.

10. Within a year's time, 46 of the 50 trees on your street die.

11. Two-thirds of the hamburgers sold in your lunchroom last week were burned.

12. Your car runs out of gas 30 miles from the nearest gas station.

13. The new record album you opened has a three-inch scratch.

14. Your new stereo is out of tune three days after you buy it.

Making a Pro-Con Chart

1. As a group, brainstorm an unduplicated list of items.

2. Individually, select the top three items and write two advantages (pros) for selecting each.

3. As a group, list the items and the pro arguments each member chose.

4. Individually, select three of the items listed and give two cons countering the pros already listed. You may not offer cons to other items unless you also offer cons to your own ideas!

5. As a group, list each member's cons in turn.

6. As a group, vote to select the top three items from the pro-con chart.

ITEM	PROS	CONS

Evaluation of Skills:
Analyzing for Cause and Effect

1. Explain each of these terms:

   a. effect
   b. probable cause

2. Explain the steps in making a causal analysis.

3. Listen to this story (or another story): Once upon a time there were three little pigs. A wolf came along. Since he hadn't eaten, he was hungry. At the first house, which was made of straw, he knocked. When the pig didn't answer, he huffed and puffed until the house fell in. Because the first pig had no house, he ran next door to his brother's house. The door was locked. The wolf grabbed him and ate him up.

   a. Make a time line and place the events from the story in chronological order.

   b. Make a list of the four causal statements in the story and note their immediate effects.

   c. Identify the final effect.

4. When would a causal analysis help you? When would it not be so helpful? What might be difficult/easy in doing your analysis?

THE CREATIVE PEOPLE SEARCH:
A TREASURE HUNT

1. Fill in each box with a signature.

2. No more than one signature by a person on your sheet.

3. This will take about five minutes. Sit down when your sheet is full.

FIND SOMEONE WHO...

baked a cake	won a prize	found a lost key
_____	_____	_____

painted a picture	stopped a fight	likes to experiment
_____	_____	_____

wrote a song or poem	invented _____	is a dreamer
_____	_____	_____

has a good imagination	likes to solve math problems	hates canned TV shows
_____	_____	_____

The Problem Scenarios

I. Mary and Sue grew up together and have been close friends for more than a dozen years. For the past two years, Barry and Sue have dated regularly. Barry has taken a sudden, heavy interest in Mary and wants her to go to the Homecoming Dance with him. Mary keeps putting him off, but really wants to go to the dance.

II. Al likes his job stacking groceries at the local market. He has held the job for three years. He's using one-half of his weekly check to buy a used car. Because business has been so good, the manager has hired another stockboy. The manager is paying the new employee, his nephew, 20 cents more per hour than he is paying Al.

III. Rich is a straight-A student. He hopes to go to college to study premed. He has two older sisters who are already in college. His family cannot afford another full tuition and Rich is concerned that if he takes a job, his grades will suffer and hurt is chances of getting into a good premed school.

Project Planning Worksheet

Date:

Proposed Ending Date:

Activity Description:

Purpose of Activity:

Desired Outcome of Activity:

Order	Key Activities	Due Dates

VIRAL MAP

First step to a cure for colds

In their frustratingly slow effort to conquer the common cold, medical scientists decades ago learned that the world's most prevalent disorder is usually caused by any of a hundred or so different kinds of viruses. Under an electron microscope, they all look like simple fuzzy balls, but the precise architecture of these so-called rhinoviruses has remained obscure. Last week, teams of scientists from Purdue and the University of Wisconsin, Madison, reported in the journal *Nature* that they had mapped in exquisite atomic detail the structure of a human cold virus called HRV14. Their achievement marked the first time that the shape of an animal virus had been so precisely determined, and raised hopes that a cure for the common cold might be possible after all.

HRV14 is marvelously complex; its genetic material is surrounded by a 20-sided outer shell that vaguely resembles a soccer ball. The sides consist of three identical triangles, each containing three proteins on its irregular surface and one below it. On the surface proteins, the researchers discovered that the features which resemble mountaintops are actually antigens, structures that antibodies seek out and attach themselves to when attacking the virus. A "canyon" snakes between these mountaintops and is believed by scientists to be shaped specifically to fit over projections, or receptors, on the surface of human cells. The virus may use this canyon to attach itself to a receptor, as a keyhole receives a key, before attacking the cell.

Armed with this knowledge of the viral topography, scientists, at least in theory, can begin closing in on a cure for the common cold. For example, a lab-made antibody designed to slide into the canyon and block it would prevent the virus from attaching to a cell. One problem with that approach, researchers say, is that antibodies are too large to enter the canyons. But another approach is possible, involving the key (the receptor) instead of the lock (the canyon). By developing a drug that somehow coats the receptors, scientists may prevent the virus from joining the cell.

In fathoming the shape of HRV14, the Purdue and Wisconsin teams depended heavily on high technology. Using X-rays produced by Cornell University's High Energy Synchrotron Source, they passed a beam through crystallized samples of the virus. Data derived from the interactions between the X-rays and the viral atomic structure were then fed into Purdue's Cyber 205 supercomputer, which enabled the researchers to produce a detailed three-dimensional picture of the virus. In fact, the supercomputer was the hero of the project. "The final set of calculations were made in a month," said Michael Rossmann, who headed the Purdue team. Without the Cyber, "They might have taken 10 years."

Evaluation of Skills:
Analytic Problem-Solving for Solutions

1. List human characteristics that seem to indicate creative thinking. For each example, name a well-known person who exhibits that characteristic and justify your choice.

2. Elaborate on this cognitive map of the problem-solving process.

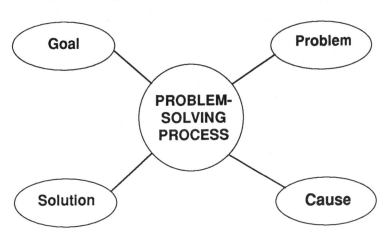

3. Write a brief expository statement about cognitive mapping. Include possible applications and pros and cons of the maps.

Worksheet Model for Original Lessons

To assist you in creating your own thinking lessons that follow the model explained in the introduction, we have included a blank worksheet which outlines the major components. Feel free to photocopy these worksheet pages. Fill them in with your own lesson content to tailor thinking lessons specifically to the needs of your class.

Lesson

Lesson Objective

Key Vocabulary

Looking Back

Getting Ready

At-A-Glance

Materials

Focus Activity

Activity Objective

Activity

Metacognitive Processing

Bibliography

Academic preparation for college. (1983). New York: The College Board

An agenda for educational renewal: A report to the secretary of education, United States Department of Education. (1984). National Consortium for Educational Excellence. Nashville, TN: Vanderbilt University, Peabody College.

Ainsworth-Land, V., & Fletcher, N. (1979). *Making waves with creative problem solving.* Buffalo, NY: D.O.K.

Alexander, C., & Cowell, J. (1983). *Mapping insights.* Learning Insights.

Anderson, L.W., & Jones, B.F. (1981). Designing instructional strategies which facilitate learning for mastery. *Educational Psychologist, 16,* 121–138.

Anderson, R., & Pearson, P.D. (1985). A schema-thoretic view of basis processes in reading comprehension. In P.D. Pearson (Ed.), *Handbook of reading research.* New York: Longman.

Anderson, R. et al. (1985). *Becoming a nation of readers.* Commission on Reading of the National Academy of Education. Springfield, IL: Phillips Bros.

Anderson, T.H., & Armbruster, B.B. (1984). Content area textbooks. In R.C. Anderson, J. Osborn, R.J. Tierney (Eds.), *Learning to read in American schools: Basal readers and content texts.* Hillsdale, NJ: Erlbaum.

Armbruster, B.B., Echols, L.H., & Brown, A.L. (1983). *The role of metacognition in reading to learn: A developmental perspective* (pp. 46-56). Urbana, IL: University of Illinois Center for the Study of Reading.

Bellanca, J. (1986). *Planning for thinking.* Palatine, IL: Skylight Publishing.

Bellanca, J. (1984). *Quality circles for educators.* Palatine, IL: Skylight Publishing.

Bellanca, J. (1984). *Skills for critical thinking.* Palatine, IL: Skylight Publishing.

Bellanca, J., & Fogarty, R. (1990). *Blueprints for thinking in the cooperative classroom.* Palatine, IL: Skylight Publishing.

Bellanca, J., & Fogarty, R. (1986). *Catch them thinking.* Palatine, IL: Skylight Publishing.

Berliner, D.C. (1984). The half-full glass: A review of research in teaching. In P.L. Hosford (Ed.), *Using what we know about teaching.* Alexandria, VA: Association for Supervision and Curriculum Development.

Beyer, B.K. (1983, November). Common sense about teaching thinking skills. *Educational Leadership,* pp. 57-62.

Beyer, B.K. (1984, March). Improving thinking skills—defining the problem. *Phi Delta Kappan,* pp. 486-490.

Biondi, A. (Ed.). (1972). *The creative process.* Buffalo, NY: D.O.K.

Black, H. and Black, S. (1981). *Figural analogies.* Pacific Grove, CA: Midwest Publications.

Bloom, B.S. (1981). *All our children learning. A primer for parents, teachers, and educators.* New York: McGraw-Hill.

Bloom, B.S. (Ed.). (1956). *Taxonomy of educational objectives: Cognitive domain.* New York: David McKay.

Brown, A.L. (1980). Metacognitive development and reading. In R.J. Spiro, B.C. Bruce, & W. F. Brewer (Eds.), *Theoretical issues in reading comprehension.* Hillsdale, NJ: Erlbaum.

Burns, M. (1976). *The book of think or how to solve a problem twice your size.* Boston, MA: Little, Brown and Company.

Campbell, T.C., Fuller, R.G., Thornton, M.C., Peter, J.L., Petterson, M.Q., Carpenter, E.T., & Narveson, R.D. (1980). A teacher's guide to the learning cycle. A Piagetian-based approach to college instruction. In R.G. Fuller, et al. (Eds.), *Piagetian programs in higher education* (pp. 27-46). Lincoln, NE: ADAPT, University of Nebraska-Lincoln.

Carnine, D., & Silbert, J. (1979). *Direct instruction reading.* Columbus, OH: Merrill Publishing.

Carpenter, E.T. (1980). Piagetian interview of college students. R.G. Fuller, et al. (Eds.), *Piagetian programs in higher education* (pp. 15-21). Lincoln, NE: ADAPT, University of Nebraska-Lincoln.

Carpenter, T.P., Corbitt, M.K., Kepner, H., Linquist, M.M., & Reys, R.W. (1980, October). Students' affective responses to mathematics: National assessment results. *Educational Leadership,* 24-37, 52, 531-539.

Chase, L. (1975). *The other side of the report card.* Glenview, IL: Scott Foresman.

Clark, B. (1979). *Growing up gifted.* Columbus, OH: Merrill Publishing.

Clement, J. (1982). Algebra word problem solutions: Thought processes underlying a common misconception. *Journal for Research in Mathematics Education, 13,* 16-30.

Clement, J. (1982). Students' preconceptions in introductory mechanics. *American Journal of Physics, 50,* 66-71.

COGITARE. (1989 to Present). The quarterly newsletter for the ASCD's Network on Teaching Thinking. Palatine, IL: Skylight Publishing.

Convigtona, M.V., Crutchfield, R.S., Davies, L., & Olton, R.M. (1974). *The productive thinking program: A course in learning to think.* Columbus, OH: Merrill Publishing.

Costa, A.L. (Ed.). (1985). *Developing minds.* Alexandria, VA: Association for Supervision and Curriculum Development.

Costa, A.L. (1984, November). Mediating the metacognitive. *Educational Leadership*, 57-62.

Costa, A.L. (1981, October). Teaching for intelligent behavior. *Educational Leadership*, 29-32.

Costa, A.L., & Lowery, L. (1989). *Techniques for teaching thinking*. Pacific Grove, CA: Midwest Publications.

Craik, F.I.M., & Lockhard, R.S. (1972). Levels of processing: Framework for memory research. *Journal of Verbal Learning and Verbal Behavior, II*, 671-684.
Creative cards: Attribute games and problems. (1966). New York: Webster Division of McGraw-Hill (ESS Science Series).

DeBoer, A.I. *The art of consulting*. Chicago, IL: Arcturus Books.

Duchastel, P.C. (1982). Textual display techniques. In D. Jonnasen (Ed.), *Principles for structuring, designing, and displaying text*. Englewood Cliffs, NJ: Educational Technology Publications.

Durkin, D. (1978-1979). What classroom observations reveal about reading comprehension instruction. *Reading Research Quarterly, 15*, 481-533.

Easterling, J., & Pasanen, J. (1979). *Confront, construct, complete*. Rochell Park, NJ: Hayden Publishing.

Eberle, B., & Stanish, B. (1980). *CPS for kids*. Buffalo, NY: D.O.K.

Eberle, B. (1982). *SCAMPER: Games for imagination development*. Buffalo, NY: D.O.K.

Eberle, B. (1982). *Visual thinking*. Buffalo, NY: D.O.K.

Edwards, B. (1979). *Drawing on the right side of the brain*. Los Angeles: J.P. Tarcher.

Eggen, Kauchak, & Harder. (1979). *Strategies for teachers*. New York: Prentice-Hall.

Elbow, P. (1973). *Writing without teachers*. New York: Oxford University Press.

Ellison, C. (1985, May 1). Science preparation of students, teachers is debated. *Education Week*, 26.

Ennis, R.H., & Norris, S.P. (1989). *Evaluating critical thinking*. Pacific Grove, CA: Midwest Publications.

Ferguson, M. (1980). *The aquarian conspiracy*. Los Angeles: J.P. Tarcher.

Feuerstein, R., & Jensen, M.R. (1980). Instructional enrichment: Theoretical bias, goals, and instruments. *The Education Form*, 401-423.

Fiestrizer, C.E. (1984). *The making of a teacher*. Washington, D.C.: National Center for Education Information.

Fiske, E. (1984, September 9). Concern over schools spurs extensive efforts at reform. *New York Times,* 1, 30.

50-state survey on critical thinking initiatives. (1985). Washington, D.C.: American Federation of Teachers.

Fogarty, R., & Bellanca, J. (1985). *Patterns for thinking—Patterns for transfer.* Palatine, IL: Skylight Publishing.

Fogarty, R., & Bellanca, J. (1986). *Teach them thinking.* Palatine, IL: Skylight Publishing.

Fogarty, R., & Haack, J. (1986). *The thinking log.* Palatine, IL: Skylight Publishing.

Fogarty, R., & Haack, J. (1988). *The thinking/writing connection.* Palatine, IL: Skylight Publishing.

Fogarty, R., & Opeka, K. (1988). *Start them thinking.* Palatine, IL: Skylight Publishing.

Gallagher, J. (1985). *Teaching the gifted child.* Boston: MA: Allyn & Bacon.

Gallelli, G. (1977). *Activity mindset guide.* Buffalo, NY: D.O.K.

Gardner, et al. (1983). *A nation at risk: The imperative for educational reform.* National Commission on Excellence in Education. Washington, DC: Department of Education.

Gifford, B.R. (1985, March 20). We must interrupt the cycle of minority-group failure. *Education Week, sec. IV,* 17-24.

Glatthorn, A. (1984). *Differentiated supervision.* Alexandria, VA: Association for Supervision and Curriculum Development.

Good, T.L. (1981, February). Teacher expectations and student perceptions. *Educational Leadership,* 415-422.

Good, T.L., & Brophy, J. E. (1984). *Looking in classrooms.* Cambridge, MA: Harper and Row.

Gordon, W.J.J. (1968). *Synectics: The development of creative capacity.* pap. 1.25 (00825, Collier) Harper and Row.

Gordon, W.J.J., & Pose, T. *Activities in metaphor.* Cambridge, MA: Porpoise Books.

Gordon, W.J.J., & Pose, T. *Teaching is listening.* Cambridge, MA: Porpoise Books.

Guilford, J.P. (1975). *Way beyond the I.Q.* Buffalo, NY: Creative Education Foundation.

Hansen, J., & Pearson, P.D. (1983). An instructional study: Improving the inferential comprehension of good and poor fourth-grade readers. *Journal of Educational Psychology, 75,* 821-829.

Harnadek, A. (1977). *Basic thinking skills: Analogies-D.* Pacific Grove, CA: Midwest Publications.

Harnadek, A. (1977). *Basic thinking skills: Patterns.* Pacific Grove, CA: Midwest, Publications.

Harnadek, A. (1980). *Critical thinking.* Pacific Grove, CA: Midwest Publications.

Herber, H.L. (1978). *Reading in the content areas: Text for teachers.* Englewood Cliffs, NJ: Prentice-Hall.

Hodgkinson, H.L. (1985). *All one system: Demography of schools, kindergarten through graduate school.* Washington, DC: Institute for Educational Leadership.

Howey, K., Matthes, W.A., & Zimpher, N.L. (1985, September). Issues and problems in professional development. Elmhurst, IL: Commissioned paper prepared for the North Central Regional Educational Laboratory.

Jenkins, J. (1974). Remember the old theory of memory? Well, forget it! *American Psychologist, 29,* 785-795.

Johnson, R. & Johnson, D. (1986). *Circles of learning: Cooperation in the classroom.* Alexandria, VA: Association for Supervision and Curriculum Development.

Johnson, R. & Johnson, D. (1987). *Learning together and alone: Cooperative, competitive, and individualistic learning.* New York: Prentice-Hall.

Jones, B.F., Amiran, M.R., & Katims, M. (1985). Teaching cognitive strategies and text structures within language arts programs. In S.F. Chipman & R. Glaser (Eds.), *Thinking and learning skills: Relating basic research to instructional practices, 1.* Hillsdale, NJ: Erlbaum.

Jones, B.F., & Spady, W.G. (1985). Enhanced mystery learning and quality of instruction. In D.V. Levine (Ed.), *Improving student achievement through mastery learning programs.* San Francisco, CA: Jossey-Bass.

Karplus, R. (1974). *Science curriculum improvement study, teachers handbook.* Berkeley, CA: University of California, Berkeley.

Larkin, J. (1983). Research on science education. In A.M. Lesgold & F. Reif (Eds.), *Education: Realizing the potential.* Washington, DC: Office of the Assisted Secretary for Educational Research and Improvement.

Larkin, J., McDermott, J., Simon, D.P., & Simon, H.A. (1980, June 20). Expert and novice performance in solving physics problems. *Science,* 1335-1342.

Maraviglia, C. (1978). *Creative problem-solving think book.* Buffalo, NY: D.O.K.

Maria, K., & McGinitie, W.H. (1982). Reading comprehension disabilities, knowledge structures, and non-accommodating text processing strategies. *Annuals of Dyslexia, 32,* 33-59.

Marcus, S., & McDonald, P. (1990). *Building a cooperative classroom.* Palatine, IL: Skylight Publishing.

Marcus, S., & McDonald, P. (1990). *Tools for the cooperative classroom.* Palatine, IL: Skylight Publishing.

Markle, S.M. (1975). They teach concepts, don't they? *Educational Researcher, 4,* 3-9.

Mayer, R.E. (1984). Aids to text comprehension. *Educational Psychologist, 19,* 30-42.

McCloskey, M., Carmazza, A., & Green, B. (1980, December 5). Curvillinear motion in the absence of external forces: Naive beliefs about the motion of objects. *Science,* 1139-1141.

The nation responds. (1984). National Commission on Excellence in Education. Washington, DC: Secretary of Education, U.S. Department of Education.

Nickerson, R.S. (1983). Computer programming as a vehicle for teaching thinking skills. *Journal of Philosophy for Children, 4,* 3-4.

Nickerson, R.S. (1982). *Understanding understanding* (BBN Report No. 5087).

Nickerson, R.S., Perkins, D.N., & Smith, E. E. (1984). *Teaching thinking* (BBN Report No. 5575).

Nickerson, R.S., Salter, W., Shepard & Herrnsteins, J. (1984). *The teaching of learning strategies* (BBN Report No. 5578).

Nisbett, R., & Ross, L. (1980). *Human inference: Strategies and shortcomings of social judgment.* Englewood Cliffs, NJ: Prentice-Hall.

Noller, R. (1977). *Scratching the surface of creative problem-solving: A bird's-eye view of CPS.* Buffalo, NY: D.O.K.

Noller, R., Parnes, S., & Bioni, A. (1976). *Creative action book.* New York: Charles Scribner and Sons.

Noller, R., Treffinger, D., & Houseman, E. (1979). *It's a gas to be gifted* or *CPS for the gifted and talented.* Buffalo, NY: D.O.K.

Osborn, A.F. (1963). *Applied imagination.* New York: Charles Scribner and Sons.

Palinscar, A.S., & Brown, A.L. (1985). Reciprocal activities to promote reading with your mind. In T.L. Harris & E. Cooper (Eds.), *Reading, thinking, and concept development: Strategies for the classroom.* New York: The College Board.

Parnes, S. (1975). *Aha! Insights into creative behavior.* Buffalo, NY: D.O.K.

Parnes, S. (1972). *Creativity: Unlocking human potential.* Buffalo, NY: D.O.K.

Pearson, P.D., & Leys, M. (1985). Teaching comprehension. In T.L. Harris & E. Cooper (Eds.), *Reading, thinking, and concept development: Strategies for the classroom.* New York: The College Board.

Perkins, D., & Swartz, R. (1989). *Teaching thinking: Issues and approaches.* Pacific Grove, CA: Midwest Publications.

Peters, T. & Austin, N. (1985). *Passion for excellence.* New York: Random House.

Peters, T. & Waterman, R., Jr. (1982). *In search of excellence*. New York: Warner Communication.

Polette, N. (1981). *Exploring books for gifted programs*. Metuchen, NJ: Scarecrow Press.

Raths, L. (1967). *Teaching for thinking*. Columbus, OH: Merrill Publishing.

Resnick, L.B. (1984). Cognitive science as educational research: Why we need it now. In *Improving education: Perspectives on educational research*. Pittsburgh, PA: University of Pittsburgh, Learning Research and Development Center.

Rico, G.L. (1983). *Writing the natural way*. Los Angeles, CA: J.P. Tarcher.

Rohwer, W.D. Jr. (1971). Prime time for education: Early childhood or adolescence? *Harvard Educational Review, 41,* 316-341.

Rosenshine, B. (1983). Teaching functions in instructional programs. *Elementary School Journal, 83,* 335-351.

Rosenshine, B., Harnischfeger, A., & Wallberg, H. (1985, March). *Classroom programs for school improvement*. Elmhurst, IL: An Advisory paper for the North Central Regional Educational Laboratory.

Rowe, M.B. (1969). Science, silence and sanctions. *Science & Children, 6,* 11-13.

Rumelhart, D.E. (1980). Schemata: The building blocks of cognition. In R.J. Spiro, B.C. Bruce & W.F. Brewer (Eds.), *Theoretical issues in reading comprehension*. Hillsdale, NJ: Erlbaum.

Scardamalia, M., Bereiter, C., & Fillion B. (1979). *The little red writing book: A source book of consequential writing activities*. Ontario, Canada: Pedagogy of Writing Project, O.I.S.E.

Schallert, D.L. (1980). The role of illustrations in reading comprehension. In R.J. Spiro, B.C. Bruce & W. F. Brewer (Eds.), *Theoretical issues in reading comprehension*. Hillsdale, NJ: Erlbaum.

Schoenfeld, A.H. (1980). Teaching problem-solving skills. *American Mathematical Monthly, 87*(10), 794-805.

Shuell, T.J. (1984, October). The concept of learning in modern-day cognitive psychology. Ellenville, New York: Paper presented at the annual meeting of the Northeastern ducational Research Association.

Shulman, L.S. (1984). Understanding pedagogy: Research for the improvement of teaching and teacher education. In *Improving education: Perspectives on educational research*. Pittsburgh, PA: University of Pittsburgh, Learning Research and Development Center.

Sirkin, J.R. (1985, May 8). All-black education agenda advocated: Press for excellence seen at odds with equity goal. *Education Week, sec. IV,* 1, 27.

Snyder, D.P. (1985). *The strategic context of education in America* (Future-Research Tech. Rep.). Washington, DC: National Education Association, Professional and Organization Development/Office of Planning.

Spiro, R. (1980). Constructive processes in prose comprehension and recall. In R.J. Spiro, B.C. Bruce, & W.F. Brewer (Eds.), *Theoretical issues in reading comprehension.* Hillsdale, NJ: Erlbaum.

Sternberg, R.J. (1981, October). Intelligence as thinking and learning skills. *Educational Leadership,* 18-21.

Task Force on Education for Economic Growth. (1983). *Action for excellence: A comprehensive plan to improve our nation's schools.* Washington, DC: Education Commission of the United States.

Teacher preparation: The anatomy of a college degree. (1985). Atlanta, GA: The Southern Regional Education Board.

Tolkien, J.R.R. (1937). *The hobbit.* New York: Ballantine Books.

Torrance, E.P. (1979). *The search for satori and creativity.* Buffalo, NY: Creative Education Foundation and Great Neck, NY: Creative Synergetics Associates.

Trowbridge, D.E., & McDermott, L.C. (1980). Investigation of student understanding of the concept of velocity in one dimension. *American Journal of Physics, 48*(12), 1010-1028.

Tversky, A., & Kahneman, D. (1974, September 27). Judgment under uncertainty: Heuristics and biases. *Science,* 1124-1131.

Underwood, V.L. (1982). *Self-management skills for college students: A program in how to learn.* Unpublished doctoral dissertation, University of Texas.

von Oech, R. (1983). *A whack on the side of the head.* New York: Warner Books.

Who's keeping score? (1980). National Institute of Education. Washington, DC: McLeod Corporation.

Notes

Notes

Notes

Notes

Additional resources to increase your teaching expertise...